CAMBRIDGE LIBRARY COLLECTION

Books of enduring scholarly value

History

The books reissued in this series include accounts of historical events and movements by eye-witnesses and contemporaries, as well as landmark studies that assembled significant source materials or developed new historiographical methods. The series includes work in social, political and military history on a wide range of periods and regions, giving modern scholars ready access to influential publications of the past.

The Life of the Fields

Richard Jefferies (1848–87) remains one of the most thoughtful and most lyrical writers on the English countryside. He had aspirations to make a living as a novelist, but it was his short factually-based articles for *The Live Stock Journal* and other magazines, drawn from a wealth of knowledge of the rural community into which he had been born, which, when brought together in book form, brought him recognition (though not wealth) and which continued to be read and admired after his early death. This volume, first published in 1884, contains a collection of essays and articles previously published during his career. Written in Jefferies' highly descriptive style, these essays describe rural life and nature in England, illustrating folk traditions and important natural events in rural communities. The sense of wonder evoked by the natural world, which permeates all of Jefferies' works, is fully exemplified in this volume.

The Life of the Fields

RICHARD JEFFERIES

CAMBRIDGE
UNIVERSITY PRESS

CAMBRIDGE UNIVERSITY PRESS

Cambridge, New York, Melbourne, Madrid, Cape Town, Singapore,
São Paolo, Delhi, Dubai, Tokyo, Mexico City

Published in the United States of America by Cambridge University Press, New York

www.cambridge.org
Information on this title: www.cambridge.org/9781108025331

© in this compilation Cambridge University Press 2010

This edition first published 1884
This digitally printed version 2010

ISBN 978-1-108-02533-1 Paperback

THE LIFE OF THE FIELDS

a

THE
LIFE OF THE FIELDS

By RICHARD JEFFERIES

AUTHOR OF "THE GAMEKEEPER AT HOME," "NATURE NEAR LONDON," "RED
DEER," "THE STORY OF MY HEART : MY AUTOBIOGRAPHY," ETC.

London
CHATTO AND WINDUS, PICCADILLY
1884

NOTE.

My thanks are due to those Editors who have so kindly permitted me to reprint the following pages:—"The Field-Play" appeared in *Time*; "Bits of Oak Bark" and "The Pageant of Summer," in *Longman's Magazine*; "Meadow Thoughts" and "Mind under Water," in *The Graphic*; "Clematis Lane," "Nature near Brighton," "Sea, Sky, and Down," "January in the Sussex Woods," and "By the Exe," in *The Standard*; "Notes on Landscape Painting," in *The Magazine of Art*; "Village Miners," in *The Gentleman's Magazine*; "Nature and the Gamekeeper," "The Sacrifice to Trout," "The Hovering of the Kestrel," and "Birds Climbing the Air," in *The St. James's Gazette*; "Sport and Science," in *The National Review*; "The Water-Colley," in *The Manchester Guardian*; "Country Literature," "Sunlight in a London Square," "Venice in the East End," "The Pigeons at the British Museum," and "The Plainest City in Europe," in *The Pall Mall Gazette*.

RICHARD JEFFERIES.

CONTENTS.

viii   *CONTENTS.*

THE LIFE OF THE FIELDS.

THE FIELD-PLAY.

I. Uptill-a-Thorn.

> " Save the nightingale alone ;
> She, poor bird, as all forlorn,
> Lean'd her breast uptill a thorn."
>
> *Passionate Pilgrim.*

She pinned her torn dress with a thorn torn from the
bushes through which she had scrambled to the hay-
field. The gap from the lane was narrow, made more
narrow by the rapid growth of summer; her rake
caught in an ash-spray, and in releasing it she
" ranted " the bosom of her print dress. So soon as
she had got through she dropped her rake on the hay,
searched for a long, nail-like thorn, and thrust it
through, for the good-looking, careless hussy never
had any provision of pins about her. Then, taking a
June rose which pricked her finger, she put the flower
by the " rant," or tear, and went to join the rest of the
hay-makers. The blood welled up out of the scratch
in the finger more freely than would have been sup-

B

posed from so small a place. She put her lips to it to
suck it away, as folk do in all quarters of the earth yet
discovered, being one of those instinctive things which
come without teaching. A red dot of blood stained
her soft white cheek, for, in brushing back her hair with
her hand, she forgot the wounded finger. With red
blood on her face, a thorn and a rose in her bosom, and
a hurt on her hand, she reached the chorus of rakers.

The farmer and the sun are the leading actors, and
the hay-makers are the chorus, who bear the burden
of the play. Marching, each a step behind the other,
and yet in a row, they presented a slanting front, and
so crossed the field, turning the " wallows." At the
hedge she took her place, the last in the row. There
were five men and eight women; all flouted her. The
men teased her for being late again at work; she said
it was so far to come. The women jeered at her
for tearing her dress—she couldn't get through a
" thornin' " hedge right. There was only one thing
she could do, and that was to "make a vool of zum
veller " (make a fool of some fellow). Dolly did not
take much notice, except that her nervous temperament showed slight excitement in the manner she
used her rake, now turning the hay quickly, now
missing altogether, then catching the teeth of the rake
in the buttercup-runners. The women did not fail to
tell her how awkward she was. By-and-by Dolly
bounced forward, and, with a flush on her cheek, took
the place next to the men. They teased her too, you
see, but there was no spiteful malice in their tongues.
There are some natures which, naturally meek, if
much condemned, defy that condemnation, and will-

ingly give it ground of justification by open guilt. The women accused her of too free a carriage with the men; she replied by seeking their company in the broad glare of the summer day. They laughed loudly, joked, but welcomed her; they chatted with her gaily; they compelled her to sip from their ale as they paused by the hedge. By noon there was a high colour on her cheeks; the sun, the exercise, the badinage had brought it up.

So fair a complexion could not brown even in summer, exposed to the utmost heat. The beams indeed did heighten the hue of her cheeks a little, but it did not shade to brown. Her chin and neck were wholly untanned, white and soft, and the blue veins roamed at their will. Lips red, a little full perhaps; teeth slightly prominent but white and gleamy as she smiled. Dark brown hair in no great abundance, always slipping out of its confinement and straggling, now on her forehead, and now on her shoulders, like wandering bines of bryony. The softest of brown eyes under long eyelashes; eyes that seemed to see everything in its gentlest aspect, that could see no harm anywhere. A ready smile on the face, and a smile in the form. Her shape yielded so easily at each movement that it seemed to smile as she walked. Her nose was the least pleasing feature—not delicate enough to fit with the complexion, and distinctly upturned, though not offensively. But it was not noticed; no one saw anything beyond the laughing lips, the laughing shape, the eyes that melted so near to tears. The torn dress, the straggling hair, the tattered shoes, the unmended stocking, the straw hat split, the mingled poverty and carelessness—perhaps rather dreaminess—disappeared when once you had met the full untroubled gaze of those beautiful eyes. Untroubled, that is, with any ulterior thought of evil or cunning; they were as open as the day, the day which you can make your own for evil or good. So, too, like the day, was she ready to the making.

No stability; now fast in motion; now slow; now by fits and starts; washing her face to-day, her hands to-morrow. Never going straight, even along the road; talking with the waggoner, helping a child to pick watercress, patting the shepherd's dog, finding a flower, and late every morning at the hay-field. It was so· far to· come, she said; no doubt it was, if these stoppings and doublings were counted in. No character whatever, no more than the wind; she was like a well-hung gate swinging to a touch; like water yielding to let a reed sway; like a singing-flame rising and falling to a word, and even to an altered tone of voice. A word pushed her this way; a word pushed her that. Always yielding, sweet, and gentle. Is not this the most seductive of all characters in women?

Had they left her alone, would it have been any different? Those bitter, coarse, feminine tongues which gave her the name of evil, and so led her to openly announce that, as she had the name, she would carry on the game. That is an old country saying, "Bear the name, carry the game." If you have the name of a poacher, then poach; you will be no worse off, and you will have the pleasure of the poaching. It is a serious matter, indeed, to give any one a bad name, more especially a sensitive, nervous, beautiful girl.

Under the shady oaks at luncheon the men all petted
her and flattered her in their rude way, which, rude as
it was, had the advantage of admitting of no mistake.
Two or three more men strolled up from other fields,
luncheon in hand and eating as they came, merely to
chat with her. One was a mower—a powerful fellow,
big boned, big everywhere, and heavy fisted; his chest
had been open since four o'clock that morning to the
sun, and was tanned like his face. He took her in his
mighty arms and kissed her before them all; not one
dared move, for the weight of that bone-smashing fist
was known. Big Mat drank, as all strong men do; he
fought; beyond that there was nothing against him.
He worked hard, and farmers are only too glad of a
man who will work. He was rather a favourite with
the master, and trusted. He kissed her twice, and
then went back to his work of mowing, which needs
more strength than any other country labour—a
mower is to a man what a dray-horse is to a horse.
They lingered long over the luncheon under the
shady oaks, with the great blue tile of the sky overhead, and the sweet scent of hay around them. They
lingered so long, that young Mr. Andrew came to start
them again, and found Dolly's cheeks all a-glow. The
heat and the laughter had warmed them; her cheeks
burned, in contrast to her white, pure forehead—for
her hat was off—and to the cool shade of the trees.
She lingered yet a little longer chatting with Mr.
Andrew—lingered a full half-hour—and when they
parted, she had given him a rose from the hedge.
Young Mr. Andrew was but half a farmer's son; he
was destined for a merchant's office in town; he had

been educated for it, and was only awaiting the promised opening. He was young, but no yokel; too knowing of town cunning and selfish hardness to entangle himself. Yet those soft brown eyes, that laughing shape; Andrew was very young and so was she, and the summer sun burned warm.

The blackbirds whistled the day away, and the swallows sought their nests under the eaves. The curved moon hung on the sky as the hunter's horn on the wall. Timid Wat—the hare—came ambling along the lane, and almost ran against two lovers in a recess of the bushes by an elm. Andrew, Andrew! these lips are too sweet for you; get you to your desk—that smiling shape, those shaded, soft brown eyes, let them alone. Be generous—do not awaken hopes you can never, never fulfil. The new-mown hay is scented yet more sweetly in the evening—of a summer's eve it is always too soon to go home.

The blackbirds whistled again, big Mat slew the grass from the rising to the going down of the sun— moon-daisies, sorrel, and buttercups lay in rows of swathe as he mowed. I wonder whether the man ever thought, as he reposed at noontide on a couch of grass under the hedge? Did he think that those immense muscles, that broad, rough-hewn plank of a chest of his, those vast bones encased in sinewy limbs —being flesh in its fulness—ought to have more of this earth than mere common men, and still more than thin-faced people—mere people, not men—in black coats? Did he dimly claim the rights of strength in his mind, and arrogate to himself the prerogatives of arbitrary kings? Who knows what big processes of reasoning, dim and big, passed through his mind in the summer days? Did he conclude he had a right to take what others only asked or worked for?

The sweet scent of the new-mown hay disappeared, the hay became whiter, the ricks rose higher, and were topped and finished. Hourly the year grew drier and sultry, as the time of wheat-harvest approached. Sap of spring had dried away; dry stalk of high summer remained, browned with heat. Mr. Andrew (in the country the son is always called by his Christian name, with the prefix Master or Mr.) had been sent for to London to fill the promised lucrative berth. The reapers were in the corn—Dolly tying up; big Mat slashing at the yellow stalks. Why the man worked so hard no one could imagine, unless it was for pure physical pleasure of using those great muscles. Unless, indeed, a fire, as it were, was burning in his mind, and drove him to labour to smother it, as they smother fires by beating them. Dolly was happier than ever—the gayest of the gay. She sang, she laughed, her white, gleaming teeth shone in the sun-shine; it was as if she had some secret which enabled her to defy the taunts and cruel, shameless words hurled at her, like clods of earth, by the other women. Gay she was, as the brilliant poppies who, having the sun as their own, cared for nothing else.

Till suddenly, just before the close of harvest, Dolly and Mat were missing from the field. Of course their absence was slanderously connected, but there was no known ground for it. Big Mat was found intoxicated at the tavern, from which he never moved for a fort-night, spending in one long drain of drink the lump

of money his mighty arms had torn from the sun in
the burning hours of work. Dolly was ill at home;
sometimes in her room, sometimes downstairs; but ill,
shaky and weak—ague they called it. There were
dark circles round her eyes, her chin drooped to her
breast; she wrapped herself in a shawl in all the heat.
It was some time before even the necessity of working
brought her forth again, and then her manner was
hurried and furtive; she would begin trembling all of
a minute, and her eyes filled quickly.

By degrees the autumn advanced, and the rooks
followed the ploughman. Dolly gradually recovered
something of her physical buoyancy; her former light-
heartedness never returned. Sometimes an incident
would cause a flash of the old gaiety, only for her to
sink back into subdued quietness. The change was
most noticeable in her eyes; soft and tender still,
brown and velvety, there was a deep sadness in them
—the longer she looked at you, the more it was visible.
They seemed as if her spirit had suffered some great
wrong; too great for redress, and that could only be
borne in silence.

How beautiful are beautiful eyes! Not from one
aspect only, as a picture is, where the light falls rightly
on it—the painter's point of view—they vary to every
and any aspect. The orb rolls to meet the changing
circumstance, and is adjusted to all. But a little
enquiry into the mechanism of the eyes will indicate
how wondrously they are formed. Science has dis-
pelled many illusions, broken many dreams; but here,
in the investigation of the eye, it has added to our
marvelling interest. The eye is still like the work of

a magician: it is physically divine. Besides the liquid flesh which delights the beholder, there is then the retina, the mysterious nerve which receives a thousand pictures on one surface and confuses none; and further, the mystery of the brain, which reproduces them at will, twenty years, yes, threescore years and ten, afterwards. Perhaps of all physical things, the eye is most beautiful, most divine.

Her eyes were still beautiful, but subdued and full of a great wrong. What that wrong was became apparent in the course of time. Dolly had to live with Mat, and, unhappily, not as his wife. Next harvest there was a child wrapped in a red shawl with her in the field, placed under the shocks while she worked. Her brother Bill talked and threatened—of what avail was it? The law gave no redress, and among men in these things, force is master still. There were none who could meet big Mat in fight.

Something seemed to burn in Mat like fire. Now he worked, and now he drank, but the drink which would have killed another did him no injury. He grew and flourished upon it, more bone, more muscle, more of the savage nature of original man. But there was something within on fire. Was he not satisfied even yet? Did he arrogate yet further prerogatives of kings?—prerogatives which even kings claim no longer. One day, while in drink, his heavy fist descended—he forgot his might; he did not check it, like Ulysses in the battle with Irus—and Dolly fell.

When they lifted her up, one eye was gone.

It was utterly put out, organically destroyed; no skill, no money, no loving care could restore it. The soft, brown velvet, the laugh, the tear gone for ever. The divine eye was broken—battered as a stone might be. The exquisite structure which reflected the trees and flowers, and took to itself the colour of the summer sky, was shapeless.

In the second year, Mr. Andrew came down, and one day met her in the village. He did not know her. The stoop, the dress which clothed, but responded to no curve, the sunken breast, and the sightless eye, how should he recognize these? This ragged, plain, this ugly, repellent creature—he did not know her. She spoke; Mr. Andrew hastily fumbled in his pocket, fetched out half a crown, gave it, and passed on quickly. How fortunate that he had not entangled himself!

Meantime, Mat drank and worked harder than ever, and became more morose, so that no one dared cross him, yet as a worker he was trusted by the farmer. Whatever it was, the fire in him burned deeper, and to the very quick. The poppies came and went once more, the harvest moon rose yellow and ruddy, all the joy of the year proceeded, but Dolly was like a violet over which a waggon-wheel had rolled. The thorn had gone deep into her bosom.

II. RURAL DYNAMITE.

In the cold North men eat bread of fir-bark; in our own fields the mouse, if pressed for food in winter, will gnaw the bark of sapling trees. Frost sharpens the teeth like a file, and hunger is keener than frost. If any one used to more fertile scenes had walked across

the barren meads Mr. Roberts rented as the summer
declined, he would have said that a living could only
be gained from them as the mouse gains it in frost-
time. By sharp-set nibbling and paring; by the
keenest frost-bitten meanness of living; by scraping
a little bit here, and saving another trifle yonder, a
farmer might possibly get through the year. At the
end of each year he would be rather worse off than
before, descending a step annually. He must nibble
like a frost-driven mouse to merely exist. So poor
was the soil, that the clay came to the surface, and in
wet weather a slip of the foot exposed it—the heel
cut through the veneer of turf into the cold, dead,
moist clay. Nothing grew but rushes. Every time a
horse moved over the marshy land his hoof left deep
holes which never again filled up, but remained the
year through, now puddles, full of rain water, and
now dry holes. The rain made the ground a swamp;
the sun cracked it as it does paint. Who could pay
rent for such a place?—for rushes, flags, and water.

Yet it was said, with whisper and nod, that the
tenant, Mr. Roberts, was a warm man as warm men
go after several years of bad seasons, falling prices,
and troubles of all kinds. For one thing, he hopped,
and it is noted among country folk, that, if a man
hops, he generally accumulates money. Mr. Roberts
hopped, or rather dragged his legs from rheumatics
contracted in thirty years' hardest of hard labour on
that thankless farm. Never did any man labour so
continually as he, from the earliest winter dawn when
the blackbird, with puffed feathers, still tried to
slumber in the thornbush, but could not for cold, on

till the latest summer eve, after the white barn owl had
passed round the fir copse. Both with his hands, and
with his eyes, now working, now watching, the man
ceased not, and such was his dogged pertinacity that,
like the mouse, he won a living. He did more, he
saved. At what price? At the price of a fireless
life: I mean without cheer, by denial of everything
which renders human life superior to that of the rabbit
in his burrow. No wife, no children, no niece, or any
woman to see to his comforts; no comfort and no
pleasure; a bare house and rheumatism. Bill, his
principal labourer, Dolly's brother, slept with him in
the same bed, master and man, a custom common in
old times, long since generally disused.

Yet Mr. Roberts was not without some humanism,
if such a word may be used; certainly he never gave
away a penny, but as certainly he cheated no man.
He was upright in conduct, and not unpleasant in
manner. He could not have been utterly crabbed for
this one labourer, Bill, to stay with him five and
twenty years. This was the six and twentieth year
they had dwelt there together in the gaunt, grey
lonely house, with woods around them, isolated from
the world, and without a hearth. A hearth is no
hearth unless a woman sit by it. This six and
twentieth year, the season then just ended, had been
the worst of the series; rain had spoiled the hay,
increased the payment of wages by lengthening the
time of hay-making; ruin, he declared, stared him in
the face; he supposed at last he must leave the
tenancy. And now the harvest was done, the ricks
thatched with flags from the marsh (to save straw),

the partridges were dispersed, the sportsmen having broken up the coveys, the black swifts had departed— they built every year in the grey stone slates on the lonely house—and nothing was left to be done but to tend the cattle morning and evening, to reflect on the losses, and to talk ceaselessly of the new terror which hung over the whole district.

It was rick-burning. Probably, gentlemen in London, who "sit at home at ease," imagine rick-burning a thing of the past, impossible since insurance robbed the incendiary of his sting, unheard of and extinct. Nothing of the kind. That it is not general is true, still to this day it breaks out in places, and rages with vehemence, placing the country side under a reign of terror. The thing seems inexplicable, but it is a fact; the burning of ricks and farm-sheds every now and then, in certain localities, reaches the dimensions of a public disaster.

One night from the garret window, Mr. Roberts, and Bill, his man, counted five fires visible at once. One was in full sight, not a mile distant, two behind the wood, above which rose the red glow, the other two dimly illumined the horizon on the left like a rising moon. While they watched in the dark garret the rats scampered behind them, and a white barn owl floated silently by. They counted up fourteen fires that had taken place since the beginning of the month, and now there were five together. Mr. Roberts did not sleep that night. Being so near the woods and preserves it was part of the understanding that he should not keep a gun—he took a stout staff, and went out to his hayricks, and there stayed till daylight. By

ten o'clock he was trudging into the town ; his mind
had been half-crazed with anxiety for his ricks ; he was
not insured, he had never insured, just to save the few
shillings it cost, such was the nibbling by which he
lived.   He had struggled hard and kept the secret to
himself—of the non-insurance—he foresaw that if
known he should immediately suffer.   But at the
town the insurance agent demurred to issue a policy.
The losses had been so heavy, there was no knowing
how much farther the loss might extend, for not the
slightest trace of the incendiary had yet been discovered, notwithstanding the reward offered, and this
was a new policy.   Had it been to add to an old one,
had Mr. Roberts insured in previous years, it would
have been different.   He could not do it on his own
responsibility, he must communicate with the head
office ; most likely they would do it, but he must have
their authority.   By return of post he should know.
Mr. Roberts trudged home again, with the misery of
two more nights confronting him; two more nights of
exposure to the chance of utter ruin.   If those ricks
were burned, the savings—the nibblings of his life—
were gone.   This intense, frost-bitten economy, by
which alone he had been able to prosper, now threatened to overwhelm him with destruction.

There is nothing that burns so resolutely as a hay-
rick; nothing that catches fire so easily.   Children
are playing with matches ; one holds the ignited match
till it scorches the fingers, and then drops it.   The
expiring flame touches three blades of dry grass, of hay
fallen from the rick, these flare immediately; the flame
runs along like a train of gunpowder, rushes up the

side of the rick, singeing it as a horse's coat is singed, takes the straw of the thatch which blackens into a hole, cuts its way through, the draught lifts it up the slope of the thatch, and in five minutes the rick is on fire irrecoverably. Unless beaten out at the first start, it is certain to go on. A spark from a pipe, dropped from the mouth of a sleeping man, will do it. Once well alight, and the engines may come at full speed, one five miles, one eight, two ten ; they may pump the pond dry, and lay hose to the distant brook—it is in vain. The spread of the flames may be arrested, but not all the water that can be thrown will put out the rick. The outside of the rick where the water strikes it turns black, and dense smoke arises, but the inside core continues to burn till the last piece is charred. All that can be done is to hastily cut away that side of the rick—if any remains—yet untouched, and carry it bodily away. A hay-rick will burn for hours, one huge mass of concentrated, glowing, solid fire, not much flame, but glowing coals, so that the farmer may fully understand, may watch and study and fully comprehend the extent of his loss. It burns itself from a square to a dome, and the red dome grows gradually smaller till its lowest layer of ashes strews the ground. It burns itself as it were in blocks : the rick was really homogeneous ; it looks while aglow as if it had been constructed of large bricks or blocks of hay. These now blackened blocks dry and crumble one by one till the dome sinks. Under·foot the earth is heated, so intense is the fire ; no one can approach, even on the windward side, within a pole's length. A widening stream of dense white smoke flows away

upwards, flecked with great sparks, blackening the
elms, and carrying flakes of burning hay over outhouses, sheds, and farmsteads. Thus from the clouds,
as it seems, drops further destruction. Nothing in the
line of the wind is safe. Fine impalpable ashes drift
and fall like rain half a mile away. Sometimes they
remain suspended in the air for hours, and come down
presently when the fire is out, like volcanic dust drifting from the crater. This dust lies soft and silky on
the hand. By the burning rick, the air rushing to the
furnace roars aloud, coming so swiftly as to be cold ;
on one side intense heat, on the other cold wind. The
pump, pump, swing, swing of the manual engines ; the
quick, short pant of the steam fire-engine ; the stream
and hiss of the water ; shouts and answers ; gleaming
brass helmets ; frightened birds ; crowds of white
faces, whose frames are in shadow ; a red glow on the
black, wet mud of the empty pond ; rosy light on the
walls of the homestead, crossed with vast magnified
shadows ; windows glistening ; men dragging sail-like
tarpaulins and rick cloths to cover the sheds ; con-
stables upright and quiet, but watchful, standing at
intervals to keep order ; if by day, the strangest
mixture of perfect calm and heated anxiety, the smoke
bluish, the floating flakes visible as black specks, the
flames tawny, pigeons fluttering round, cows grazing
in idol-like indifference to human fears. Ultimately,
rows of flattened and roughly circular layers of
blackened ashes, whose traces remain for months.

    This is dynamite in the hands of the village ruffian.

    This hay, or wheat, or barley, not only represents
money ; it represents the work of an entire year, the

sunshine of a whole summer; it is the outcome of man's thought and patient labour, and it is the food of the helpless cattle. Besides the hay, there often go with it buildings, implements, waggons, and occasionally horses are suffocated. Once now and then the farmstead goes.

Now, has not the farmer, even if covered by insurance, reason good to dread this horrible incendiarism ? It is a blow at his moral existence as well as at his pecuniary interests. Hardened indeed must be that heart that could look at the old familiar scene, blackened, fire-spilt, trodden, and blotted, without an inward desolation. Boxes and barrels of merchandise in warehouses can be replaced, but money does not replace the growth of nature.

Hence the brutality of it—the blow at a man's heart. His hay, his wheat, his cattle, are to a farmer part of his life ; coin will not replace them. Nor does the incendiary care if the man himself, his house, home, and all perish at the same time. It is dynamite in despite of insurance. The new system of silos—burying the grass when cut at once in its green state, in artificial caves—may much reduce the risk of fire if it comes into general use.

These fire invasions almost always come in the form of an epidemic; not one but three, five, ten, fifteen fires follow in quick succession. Sometimes they last through an entire winter, though often known to take place in summer, directly after harvest.

Rarely does detection happen ; to this day half these incendiary fires are never followed by punishment. Yet it is noted that they generally occur within a

c

certain radius ; they are all within six, or seven, or
eight miles, being about the distance that a man or
two bent on evil could compass in the night time.
But it is not always night ; numerous fires are started
in broad daylight. Stress of winter weather, little
food, and clothing, and less fuel at home have been put
forward as causes of a chill desperation, ending in
crime. On the contrary, these fires frequently occur
when labourers' pockets are full, just after they have
received their harvest wages. Bread is not at famine
prices; hard masters are not specially selected for the
gratification of spite; good masters suffer equally.
What then is the cause ?

There is none but that bitter, bitter feeling which
I venture to call the dynamite disposition, and which
is found in every part of the civilized world; in
Germany, Italy, France, and our own mildly ruled
England. A brooding, morose, concentrated hatred
of those who possess any kind of substance or comfort;
landlord, farmer, every one. An unsparing vendetta,
a merciless shark-like thirst of destructive vengeance ;
a monomania of battering, smashing, crushing, such as
seizes the Lancashire weaver, who kicks his woman's
brains out without any special reason for dislike,
mingled with and made more terrible by this un-
changeable hostility to property and those who own it.
No creed, no high moral hopes of the rights of man
and social regeneration, no true *sans culottism* even,
nothing at all but set teeth and inflated nostrils ; blow
up, burn, smash, annihilate ! A disposition or character which is not imaginary but a fact, as proved
abundantly by the placing of rails and iron chairs on

lines to upset trains, by the dynamite explosions at
Government offices, railway stations, and even at newspaper offices, the sending of letters filled with explo-
sives, firing dynamite in trout streams just to destroy
the harmless fish; a character which in the country has
hitherto manifested itself in the burning of ricks and
farm buildings. Science is always putting fresh power
into the hands of this class. In cities they have
partly awakened to the power of knowledge; in the
country they still use the match. If any one thinks
that there is no danger in England because there are no
deep-seated causes of discontent, such as foreign rule,
oppressive enactments, or conscription, I can assure
him that he is wofully mistaken. This class needs no
cause at all; prosperity cannot allay its hatred, and
adversity does not weaken it. It is certainly unwise
to the last degree to provoke this demon, to control
which as yet no means have been found. You cannot arrest the invisible; you cannot pour Martini-
Henry bullets into a phantom. How are you going
to capture people who blow themselves into atoms in
order to shatter the frame of a Czar?

In its dealings with the lower class this generation
is certainly far from wise. Never was the distinction
so sharp between the poor—the sullen poor who stand
scornful and desperate at the street corners—and the
well-to-do. The contrast now extends to every one
who can afford a black coat. It is not confined to the
millionaire. The contrast is with every black coat.
Those who only see the drawing-room side of society,
those who move, too, in the well-oiled atmosphere of
commercial offices, are quite ignorant of the savage

animosity which watches them to and fro the office or the drawing-room from the street corner. Question it is if any mediæval soldiery bursting abroad in Sinigaglia were so brutal as is the street rough, that blot and hideous product of modern civilization. How easy it is to point to the sobriety and the good sense of the working class and smile in assumed complacency! What have the sober mass of the working class to do with it? No more than you or I, or the Rothschilds, or dukes of blood royal. There the thing is, and it requires no great sagacity to see that the present mode of dealing with it is a failure and likely to be worse. If you have gunpowder, you should not put it under hydraulic pressure. You should not stir it up and hold matches to it to see if it is there. That is what prosecutions and imprisonments on charges of atheism and so on do. It is stirring up the powder and trying it with a match.

Nor should you put it under hydraulic pressure, which is now being done all over the country, under the new laws which force every wretch who enters a workhouse for a night's shelter to stay there two nights; under the cold-blooded cruelty which, in the guise of science, takes the miserable quarter of a pint of ale from the lips of the palsied and decrepit inmates; which puts the imbecile—even the guiltless imbecile—on what is practically bread and water. Words fail me to express the cruelty and inhumanity of this crazed legislation.

Sometimes we see a complacent paragraph in the papers, penned by an official doubtless, congratulating the public that the number relieved under the new regulations has dropped from, say, six hundred to a hundred and fifty. And what, oh blindest of the blind, do you imagine has become of the remaining four hundred and fifty? Has your precious folly extinguished them? Are they dead? No, indeed. All over the country, hydraulic pressure, in the name of science, progress, temperance, and similar perverted things, is being put on the gunpowder—or the dynamite, if you like—of society. Every now and then some individual member of the Army of Wretches turns and becomes the Devil of modern civilization. Modern civilization has put out the spiritual Devil and produced the Demon of Dynamite. Let me raise a voice, in pleading for more humane treatment of the poor—the only way, believe me, by which society can narrow down and confine the operations of this new Devil. A human being is not a dog, yet is treated worse than a dog.

Force these human dogs to learn to read with empty stomachs—stomachs craving for a piece of bread while education is crammed into them. In manhood, if unfortunate, set them to break stones. If imbecility supervene give them bread and water. In helpless age give them the cup of cold water. This is the way to breed dynamite. And then at the other end of the scale let your Thames Embankment Boulevard be the domain of the street rough; let your Islington streets be swept by bands of brutes; let the well dressed be afraid to venture anywhere unless in the glare of gas and electric light! Manufacture it in one district, and give it free scope and play in another. Yet never was there an age in which the mass of society, from the

titled to the cottager, was so full of real and true
humanity, so ready to start forward to help, so im-
bued with the highest sentiments. The wrong is done
in official circles. No steel-clad baron of Norman
days, no ruthless red-stockinged cardinal, with the
Bastile in one hand and the tumbril in the other, ever
ruled with so total an absence of Heart as the modern
" official," the Tyrants of the nineteenth century;
whose rods are hobbies in the name of science mis-
called, in the name of temperance perverted, in the
name of progress backwards, in the name of education
without food. It is time that the common sense of
society at large rose in revolution against it. Meantime dynamite.

This is a long digression : suppose while you have
been reading it that Mr. Roberts has passed one of
the two terrible nights, his faithful Bill at one end of
the rickyard and himself at the other. The second
night they took up their positions in the same manner
as soon as it was dark. There was no moon, and the
sky was overcast with those stationary clouds which
often precede a great storm, so that the darkness was
marked, and after they had parted a step or two they
lost sight of each other. Worn with long wakefulness,
and hard labour during the day, they both dropped
asleep at their posts. Mr. Roberts awoke from the
dead vacancy of sleep to the sensation of a flash of
light crossing his eyelids, and to catch a glimpse of a
man's neck with a red necktie illuminated by flame
like a Rembrandt head in the centre of shadow. He
leaped forward literally yelling—the incendiary he
wholly forgot—his rick! his rick! He beat the side

of the rick with his stick, and as it had but just caught he beat the flame out. Then he dropped senseless on the ground. Bill, awakened by Roberts' awful yell or shriek of excitement, started to his feet, heard a man rushing by in the darkness, and hurled his heavy stick in that direction. By the thud which followed and a curse, he knew it had hit the object, but not with sufficient force to bring the scoundrel down. The fellow escaped; Bill went to his master and lifted him up; how he got Roberts home he did not know, but it was hours before Roberts could speak. Towards sunrise he recovered, and would go immediately to assure himself that the ricks were safe. Then they found a man's hat—Bill's stick had knocked it off—and by that hat and the red necktie the incendiary was brought to justice. The hat was big Mat's; he always wore a red necktie.

Big Mat made no defence; he was simply stolidly indifferent to the whole proceedings. The only statement he made was that he had not fired four of the ricks, and he did not know who had done so. Example is contagious; some one had followed the dynamite lead, detection never took place, but the fires ceased. Mat, of course, went for the longest period of penal servitude the law allotted.

I should say that he did not himself know why he did it. That intense, brooding moroseness, that wormwood hatred, does not often understand itself. So much the more dangerous is it; no argument, no softening influence can reach it.

Faithful Bill, who had served Mr. Roberts almost all his life, and who probably would have served him till the end, received a money reward from the insurance office for his share in detecting the incendiary. This reward ruined him—killed him. Golden sovereigns in his pocket destroyed him. He went on the drink; he drank, and was enticed to drink, till in six weeks he died in the infirmary of the workhouse.

Mat being in the convict prison, and Dolly near to another confinement, she could not support herself; she was driven to the same workhouse in which her brother had but just died. I am not sure, but believe that pseudo-science, the Torturer of these days, denied her the least drop of alcohol during her travail. If it did permit one drop, then was the Torturer false to his creed. Dolly survived, but utterly broken, hollow-chested, a workhouse fixture. Still, so long as she could stand she had to wash in the laundry; weak as she was, they weakened her still farther with steam and heat, and labour. Washing is hard work for those who enjoy health and vigour. To a girl, broken in heart and body, it is a slow destroyer. Heat relaxes all the fibres; Dolly's required bracing. Steam will soften wood and enable the artificer to bend it to any shape. Dolly's chest became yet more hollow; her cheek-bones prominent; she bent to the steam. This was the girl who had lingered in the lane to help the boy pick watercress, to gather a flower, to listen to a thrush, to bask in the sunshine. Open air and green fields were to her life itself. Heart miseries are always better borne in the open air. How just, how truly scientific, to shut her in a steaming wash-house!

The workhouse was situated in a lovely spot, on

the lowest slope of hills, hills covered afar with woods. Meads at hand, corn fields farther away, then green slopes over which broad cloud-shadows glided slowly. The larks sang in spring, in summer the wheat was golden, in autumn the distant woods were brown and red and yellow. Had you spent your youth in those fields, had your little drama of life been enacted in them, do you not think that you would like at least to gaze out at them from the windows of your prison? It was observed that the miserable wretches were always looking out of the windows in this direction. The windows on that side were accordingly built up and bricked in that they might not look out.

BITS OF OAK BARK.

I. The Acorn-Gatherer.

BLACK rooks, yellow oak leaves, and a boy asleep
at the foot of the tree. His head was lying on a
bulging root close to the stem : his feet reached to a
small sack or bag half full of acorns. In his slumber
his forehead frowned—they were fixed lines, like the
grooves in the oak bark. There was nothing else in
his features attractive or repellent : they were such as
might have belonged to a dozen hedge children. The
set angry frown was the only distinguishing mark—
like the dents on a penny made by a hobnail boot, by
which it can be known from twenty otherwise precisely similar. His clothes were little better than
sacking, but clean, tidy, and repaired. Any one would
have said, "Poor, but carefully tended." A kind heart
might have put a threepenny-bit in his clenched little
fist, and sighed. But that iron set frown on the young
brow would not have unbent even for the silver. Caw !
Caw !

The happiest creatures in the world are the rooks
at the acorns. It is not only the eating of them but
the finding : the fluttering up there and hopping from

branch to branch, the sidling out to the extreme end
of the bough, and the inward chuckling when a friend
lets his acorn drop tip-tap from bough to bough.
Amid such plenty they cannot quarrel or fight, having
no cause of battle, but they can boast of success, and
do so to the loudest of their voices. He who has
selected a choice one flies with it as if it were a nugget
in his beak, out to some open spot of ground, followed
by a general Caw!

This was going on above while the boy slept below.
A thrush looked out from the hedge, and among the
short grass there was still the hum of bees, constant
sun-worshippers as they are. The sunshine gleamed
on the rooks' black feathers overhead, and on the sward
sparkled from hawkweed, some lotus and yellow weed,
as from a faint ripple of water. The oak was near a
corner formed by two hedges, and in the angle was a
narrow thorny gap. Presently an old woman, very
upright, came through this gap carrying a faggot on
her shoulder and a stout ash stick in her hand. She
was very clean, well dressed for a labouring woman,
hard of feature, but superior in some scarcely defined
way to most of her class. The upright carriage had
something to do with it, the firm mouth, the light blue
eyes that looked every one straight in the face. Possibly these, however, had less effect than her conscious
righteousness. Her religion lifted her above the rest,
and I do assure you that it was perfectly genuine.
That hard face and cotton gown would have gone to
the stake.

When she had got through the gap she put the
faggot down in it, walked a short distance out into

the field, and came back towards the boy, keeping him between her and the corner. Caw! said the rooks, Caw! Caw! Thwack, thwack, bang, went the ash stick on the sleeping boy, heavily enough to have broken his bones. Like a piece of machinery suddenly let loose, without a second of dubious awakening and without a cry, he darted straight for the gap in the corner. There the faggot stopped him, and before he could tear it away the old woman had him again, thwack, thwack, and one last stinging slash across his legs as he doubled past her. Quick as the wind as he rushed he picked up the bag of acorns and pitched it into the mound, where the acorns rolled down into a pond and were lost—a good round shilling's worth. Then across the field, without his cap, over the rising ground, and out of sight. The old woman made no attempt to hold him, knowing from previous experience that it was useless, and would probably result in her own overthrow. The faggot, brought a quarter of a mile for the purpose, enabled her, you see, to get two good chances at him.

A wickeder boy never lived: nothing could be done with the reprobate. He was her grandson— at least, the son of her daughter, for he was not legitimate. The man drank, the girl died, as was believed, of sheer starvation: the granny kept the child, and he was now between ten and eleven years old. She had done and did her duty, as she understood it. A prayer-meeting was held in her cottage twice a week, she prayed herself aloud among them, she was a leading member of the sect. Neither example, precept, nor the rod could change that boy's heart. In time perhaps she got to beat him from habit rather than from any particular anger of the moment, just as she fetched water and filled her kettle, as one of the ordinary events of the day. Why did not the father interfere? Because if so he would have had to keep his son: so many shillings a week the less for ale.

In the garden attached to the cottage there was a small shed with a padlock, used to store produce or wood in. One morning, after a severe beating, she drove the boy in there and locked him in the whole day without food. It was no use, he was as hardened as ever.

A footpath which crossed the field went by the cottage, and every Sunday those who were walking to church could see the boy in the window with granny's Bible open before him. There he had to sit, the door locked, under terror of stick, and study the page. What was the use of compelling him to do that? He could not read. "No," said the old woman, "he won't read, but I makes him look at his book."

The thwacking went on for some time, when one day the boy was sent on an errand two or three miles, and for a wonder started willingly enough. At night he did not return, nor the next day, nor the next, and it was as clear as possible that he had run away. No one thought of tracking his footsteps, or following up the path he had to take, which passed a railway, brooks, and a canal. He had run away, and he might stop away: it was beautiful sumner weather and it would do him no harm to stop out for a week. A dealer who had business in a field by the canal thought indeed that he saw something in the water, but he

did not want any trouble, nor indeed did he know
that some one was missing. Most likely a dead dog ;
so he turned his back and went to look again at the
cow he thought of buying. A barge came by, and
the steerswoman, with a pipe in her mouth, saw something roll over and come up under the rudder : the
length of the barge having passed over it. She knew
what it was, but she wanted to reach the wharf and
go ashore and have a quart of ale. No use picking
it up, only make a mess on deck, there was no reward
—"Gee-up ! Neddy." The barge went on, turning up
the mud in the shallow water, sending ripples washing
up to the grassy meadow shores, while the moorhens
hid in the flags till it was gone. In time a labourer
walking on the towing-path saw "it," and fished it out,
and with it a slender ash sapling, with twine and
hook, a worm still on it. This was why the dead boy
had gone so willingly, thinking to fish in the " river,"
as he called the canal. When his feet slipped and he
fell in, his fishing-line somehow became twisted about
his arms and legs, else most likely he would have
scrambled out, as it was not very deep. This was
the end ; nor was he even remembered. Does any
one sorrow for the rook, shot, and hung up as a scarecrow ? The boy had been talked to, and held up as
a scarecrow all his life : he was dead, and that is all.
As for granny, she felt no twinge : she had done her
duty.

II. The Legend of a Gateway.

A great beech tree with a white mark some way
up the trunk stood in the mound by a gate which

opened into a lane. Strangers coming down the lane in the dusk often hesitated before they approached this beech. The white mark looked like a ghostly figure emerging from the dark hedge and the shadow of the tree. The trunk itself was of the same hue at that hour as the bushes, so that the whiteness seemed to stand out unsupported. So perfect was the illusion that even those who knew the spot well, walking or riding past and not thinking about it, started as it suddenly came into sight. Ploughboys used to throw flints at it, as if the sound of the stone striking the tree assured them that it was really material. Some lichen was apparently the cause of this whiteness: the great beech indeed was known to be decaying and was dotted with knot-holes high above. The gate was rather low, so that any one could lean with arms over the top bar.

At one time a lady used to be very frequently seen just inside the gate, generally without a hat, for the homestead was close by. Sometimes a horse, saddled and bridled, but without his rider, was observed to be fastened to the gate, and country people, being singularly curious and inquisitive, if they chanced to go by always peered through every opening in the hedge till they had discerned where the pair were walking among the cowslips. More often a spaniel betrayed them, especially in the evening, for while the courting was proceeding he amused himself digging with his paws at the rabbit-holes in the mound. The folk returning to their cottages at even smiled and looked meaningly at each other if they heard a peculiarly long and shrill whistle, which was known to every

one as Luke's signal. Some said that it was heard
every evening : no matter how far Luke had to ride
in the day, his whistle was sure to be heard towards
dusk.   Luke was a timber-dealer, or merchant, a calling that generally leads to substantial profit as wealth
is understood in country places. He bought up likely
timber all over the neighbourhood : he had wharves
on the canal, and yards by the little railway station
miles away.   He often went up to "Lunnon," but
if it was ninety miles, he was sure to be back in time
to whistle.   If he was not too busy the whistle used
to go twice a day, for when he started off in the morning, no matter where he had to go to, that lane was
the road to it.   The lane led everywhere.

Up in the great beech about eleven o'clock on
spring mornings there was always a wood-pigeon.
The wood-pigeon is a contemplative sort of bird, and
pauses now and then during the day to consider over
his labours in filling his crop.   He came again about
half-past four, but it was at eleven that his visit to
the beech was usually noticed.   From the window in
the lady's own room the beech and the gate could be
seen, and as that was often Luke's time she frequently
sat upstairs with the window open listening for the
sound of hoofs, or the well-known whistle.   She saw
the wood-pigeon on so many occasions that at last
she grew to watch for the bird, and when he went
up into the tree, put down her work or her book and
walked out that way.   Secure in the top of the great
beech, and conscious that it was spring, when guns
are laid aside, the wood-pigeon took no heed of her.
There is nothing so pleasant to stroll among as cow-

slips. This mead was full of them, so much so that
a little way in front the surface seemed yellow. They
had all short stalks ; this is always the case where
these flowers grow very thickly, and the bells were
a pale and somewhat lemon colour. The great cowslips with deep yellow and marked spots grow by
themselves in bunches in corners or on the banks of
brooks. Here a man might have mown acres of cowslips, pale but sweet. Out of their cups the bees
hummed as she walked amongst them, a closed book
in her hand, dreaming. She generally returned with
Luke's spaniel beside her, for whether his master came
or not the knowing dog rarely missed his visit, aware
that there was always something good for him.

One morning she went dreaming on like this
through the cowslips, past the old beech and the gate,
and along by the nut-tree hedge. It was very sunny
and warm, and the birds sang with all their might,
for there had been a shower at dawn, which always
sets their hearts a-tune. At least eight or nine of
them were singing at once, thrush and blackbird,
cuckoo (afar off), dove, and greenfinch, nightingale,
robin and loud wren, and larks in the sky. But,
unlike all other music, though each had a different
voice and the notes crossed and interfered with each
other, yet they did not jangle but produced the
sweetest sounds. The more of them that sang together, the sweeter the music. It is true they all had
one thought of love at heart, and that perhaps brought
about the concord. She did not expect to see Luke
that morning, knowing that he had to get some felled
trees removed from a field, the farmer wishing them

taken away before the mowing-grass grew too high, and as the spot was ten or twelve miles distant he had to start early. Not being so much on the alert, she fell deeper perhaps into reverie, which lasted till she reached the other side of the field, when the spaniel rushed out of the hedge and leaped up to be noticed, quite startling her. At the same moment she thought she heard the noise of hoofs in the lane— it might be Luke—and immediately afterwards there came his long, shrill, and peculiar whistle from the gate under the beech. She ran as fast as she could, the spaniel barking beside her, and was at the gate in two or three minutes, but Luke was not there. Nor was he anywhere in the lane—she could see up and down it over the low gate. He must have gone on up to the homestead, not seeing her. At the house, however, she found they had not seen him. He had not called. A little hurt that he should have galloped on so hastily, she set about some household affairs, resolved to think no more of him that morning, and to give him a frown when he came in the evening. But he did not come in the evening; it was evident he was detained.

Luke's trees were lying in the long grass beside a copse, and the object was to get them out of the field, across the adjacent railway, and to set them down in a lane, on the sward, whence he could send for them at leisure. The farmer was very anxious to get them out of the grass, and Luke did his best to oblige him. When Luke arrived at the spot, having for once ridden straight there, he found that almost all the work was done, and only one tree remained.

This they were getting up on the timber-carriage, and Luke dismounted and assisted. While it was on the timber-carriage, he said, as it was the last, they could take it along to the wharf. The farmer had come down to watch how the work got on, and with him was his little boy, a child of five or six. When the boy saw the great tree fixed, he cried to be mounted on it for a ride, but as it was so rough they persuaded him to ride on one of the horses instead. As they all approached the gate at the level crossing, a white gate with the words in long black letters, "To be kept Locked," they heard the roar of the morning express and stayed for it to go by. So soon as the train had passed, the gate was opened and the horses began to drag the carriage across. As they strained at the heavy weight, the boy found the motion uncomfortable and cried out, and Luke, always kind-hearted, went and held him on. Whether it was the shouting at the team, the cracking of the whip, the rumbling of the wheels, or what, was never known; but suddenly the farmer, who had crossed the rail, screamed, "The goods!" Round the curve by the copse, and till then hidden by it, swept a goods train, scarce thirty yards away. Luke might have saved himself, but the boy! He snatched the child from the horse, hurled him—literally hurled him —into the father's arms, and in the instant was a shapeless mass. The scene is too dreadful for further description. This miserable accident happened, as the driver of the goods train afterwards stated, at exactly eight minutes past eleven o'clock.

It was precisely at that time that Luke's lady, dreaming among the cowslips, heard the noise of hoofs, and his long, shrill and peculiar whistle at the gate beneath the beech. She was certain of the time, for these reasons : first, she had seen the wood-pigeon go up into the beech just before she started out; secondly, she remembered nodding to an aged labourer who came up to the house every morning at that hour for his ale; thirdly, it would take a person walking slowly eight or ten minutes to cross that side of the mead ; and, fourthly, when she came back to the house to see if Luke was there, the clock pointed to a quarter past, and was known to be a little fast. Without a doubt she had heard the well-known whistle, apparently coming from the gate beneath the beech exactly at the moment poor Luke was dashed to pieces twelve miles away.

III. A Roman Brook.

The brook has forgotten me, but I have not forgotten the brook. Many faces have been mirrored since in the flowing water, many feet have waded in the sandy shallow. I wonder if any one else can see it in a picture before the eyes as I can, bright, and vivid as trees suddenly shown at night by a great flash of lightning. All the leaves and branches and the birds at roost are visible during the flash. It is barely a second; it seems much longer. Memory, like the lightning, reveals the pictures in the mind. Every curve, and shore, and shallow is as familiar now as when I followed the winding stream so often. When the mowing-grass was at its height, you could not walk far beside the bank; it grew so thick and

strong and full of umbelliferous plants as to weary the
knees. The life as it were of the meadows seemed to
crowd down towards the brook in summer, to reach
out and stretch towards the life-giving water. There
the buttercups were taller and closer together, nails of
gold driven so thickly that the true surface was not
visible. Countless rootlets drew up the richness of
the earth like miners in the darkness, throwing their
petals of yellow ore broadcast above them. With
their fulness of leaves the hawthorn bushes grow
larger—the trees extend farther—and thus overhung
with leaf and branch, and closely set about by grass
and plant, the brook disappeared only a little way off,
and could not have been known from a mound and
hedge. It was lost in the plain of meads—the flowers
alone saw its sparkle.

Hidden in those bushes and tall grasses, high in the
trees and low on the ground there were the nests of
happy birds. In the hawthorns blackbirds and thrushes
built, often overhanging the stream, and the fledglings
fluttered out into the flowery grass. Down among the
stalks of the umbelliferous plants, where the grasses
were knotted together, the nettle-creeper concealed
her treasure, having selected a hollow by the bank so
that the scythe should pass over. Up in the pollard
ashes and willows here and there wood-pigeons built.
Doves cooed in the little wooded enclosures where the
brook curved almost round upon itself. If there was
a hollow in the oak a pair of starlings chose it, for
there was no advantageous nook that was not seized
on. Low beside the willow stoles the sedge-reedlings
built; on the ledges of the ditches, full of flags, moor-

hens made their nests. After the swallows had coursed
long miles over the meads to and fro, they rested on
the tops of the ashes and twittered sweetly. Like the
flowers and grass, the birds were drawn towards the
brook.   They built by it, they came to it to drink; in
the evening a grasshopper-lark trilled in a hawthorn
bush.   By night crossing the footbridge a star sometimes shone in the water underfoot. At morn and
even the peasant girls came down to dip; their path
was worn through the mowing-grass, and there was a
flat stone let into the bank as a step to stand on.
Though they were poorly habited, without one line of
form or tint of colour that could please the eye, there
is something in dipping water that is Greek—Homeric
—something that carries the mind home to primitive
times.   Always the little children came with them;
they too loved the brook like the grass and birds.
They wanted to see the fishes dart away and hide in
the green flags: they flung daisies and buttercups into
the stream to float and catch awhile at the flags, and
float again and pass away, like the friends of our boyhood, out of sight.   Where there was pasture roan
cattle came to drink, and horses, restless horses, stood
for hours by the edge under the shade of ash trees.
With what joy the spaniel plunged in, straight from
the bank out among the flags—you could mark his
course by seeing their tips bend as he brushed them
swimming.   All life loved the brook.

Far down away from roads and hamlets there was
a small orchard on the very bank of the stream, and
just before the grass grew too high to walk through
I looked in the enclosure to speak to its owner. He

was busy with his spade at a strip of garden, and grumbled that the hares would not let it alone, with all that stretch of grass to feed on. Nor would the rooks; and the moorhens ran over it, and the water-rats burrowed; the wood-pigeons would have the peas, and there was no rest from them all. While he talked and talked, far from the object in hand, as aged people will, I thought how the apple tree in blossom before us cared little enough who saw its glory. The branches were in bloom everywhere, at the top as well as at the side; at the top where no one could see them but the swallows. They did not grow for human admiration: that was not their purpose; that is our affair only— we bring the thought to the tree. On a short branch low down the trunk there hung the weather-beaten and broken handle of an earthenware vessel; the old man said it was a jug, one of the old folks' jugs—he often dug them up. Some were cracked, some nearly perfect; lots of them had been thrown out to mend the lane. There were some chips among the heap of weeds yonder. These fragments were the remains of Anglo-Roman pottery. Coins had been found—half a gallon of them—the children had had most. He took one from his pocket, dug up that morning; they were of no value, they would not ring. The labourers tried to get some ale for them, but could not; no one would take the little brass things. That was all he knew of the Cæsars: the apples were in fine bloom now, weren't they?

Fifteen centuries before there had been a Roman station at the spot where the lane crossed the brook. There the centurions rested their troops after their

weary march across the downs, for the lane, now
bramble-grown and full of ruts, was then a Roman
road.   There were villas, and baths, and fortifications;
these things you may read about in books.   They are
lost now in the hedges, under the flowering grass, in
the ash copses, all forgotten in the lane, and along
the footpath where the June roses will bloom after
the apple blossom has dropped.   But just where the
ancient military way crosses the brook there grow the
finest, the largest, the bluest, and most lovely forget-
me-nots that ever lover gathered for his lady.

The old man, seeing my interest in the fragments of
pottery, wished to show me something of a different
kind lately discovered.   He led me to a spot where
the brook was deep, and had somewhat undermined
the edge.   A horse trying to drink there had pushed
a quantity of earth into the stream, and exposed a
human skeleton lying within a few inches of the
water.   Then I looked up the stream and remembered
the buttercups and tall grasses, the flowers that
crowded down to the edge; I remembered the nests,
and the dove cooing; the girls that came down to
dip, the children that cast their flowers to float away.
The wind blew the loose apple bloom and it fell in
showers of painted snow.   Sweetly the greenfinches
were calling in the trees : afar the voice of the cuckoo
came over the oaks.   By the side of the living water,
the water that all things rejoiced in, near to its gentle
sound, and the sparkle of sunshine on it, had lain this
sorrowful thing.

THE PAGEANT OF SUMMER.

I.

GREEN rushes, long and thick, standing up above the edge of the ditch, told the hour of the year as distinctly as the shadow on the dial the hour of the day. Green and thick and sappy to the touch, they felt like summer, soft and elastic, as if full of life, mere rushes though they were. On the fingers they left a green scent; rushes have a separate scent of green, so, too, have ferns, very different to that of grass or leaves. Rising from brown sheaths, the tall stems enlarged a little in the middle, like classical columns, and heavy with their sap and freshness, leaned against the hawthorn sprays. From the earth they had drawn its moisture, and made the ditch dry; some of the sweetness of the air had entered into their fibres, and the rushes—the common rushes—were full of beautiful summer. The white pollen of early grasses growing on the edge was dusted from them each time the hawthorn boughs were shaken by a thrush. These lower sprays came down in among the grass, and leaves and grass-blades touched. Smooth round stems of angelica, big as a gun-barrel, hollow and strong, stood on the slope of the mound, their tiers of well-balanced branches rising like those of a tree. Such a sturdy growth pushed back the ranks of hedge parsley in full white flower, which blocked every avenue and winding bird's-path of the bank. But the "gix," or wild parsnip, reached already high above both, and would rear its fluted stalk, joint on joint, till it could face a man. Trees they were to the lesser birds, not even bending if perched on; but though so stout, the birds did not place their nests on or against them. Something in the odour of these umbelliferous plants, perhaps, is not quite liked; if brushed or bruised they give out a bitter greenish scent. Under their cover, well shaded and hidden, birds build, but not against or on the stems, though they will affix their nests to much less certain supports. With the grasses that overhung the edge, with the rushes in the ditch itself, and these great plants on the mound, the whole hedge was wrapped and thickened. No cunning of glance could see through it; it would have needed a ladder to help any one look over.

It was between the may and the June roses. The may bloom had fallen, and among the hawthorn boughs were the little green bunches that would feed the red-wings in autumn. High up the briars had climbed, straight and towering while there was a thorn or an ash sapling, or a yellow-green willow, to uphold them, and then curving over towards the meadow. The buds were on them, but not yet open; it was between the may and the rose.

As the wind, wandering over the sea, takes from each wave an invisible portion, and brings to those on shore the ethereal essence of ocean, so the air lingering among the woods and hedges—green waves and billows —became full of fine atoms of summer. Swept from notched hawthorn leaves, broad-topped oak-leaves, narrow ash sprays and oval willows; from vast elm cliffs and sharp-taloned brambles under; brushed from the waving grasses and stiffening corn, the dust of the sunshine was borne along and breathed. Steeped in flower and pollen to the music of bees and birds, the stream of the atmosphere became a living thing. It was life to breathe it, for the air itself was life. The strength of the earth went up through the leaves into the wind. Fed thus on the food of the Immortals, the heart opened to the width and depth of the summer —to the broad horizon afar, down to the minutest creature in the grass, up to the highest swallow. Winter shows us Matter in its dead form, like the Primary rocks, like granite and basalt—clear but cold and frozen crystal. Summer shows us Matter changing into life, sap rising from the earth through a million tubes, the alchemic power of light entering the solid oak; and see! it bursts forth in countless leaves. Living things leap in the grass, living things drift upon the air, living things are coming forth to breathe in every hawthorn bush. No longer does the immense weight of Matter—the dead, the crystallized—press ponderously on the thinking mind. The whole office of Matter is to feed life—to feed the green rushes, and the roses that are about to be; to feed the swallows above, and us that wander beneath them. So much greater is this green and common rush than all the Alps.

Fanning so swiftly, the wasp's wings are but just
visible as he passes ; did he pause, the light would be
apparent through their texture. On the wings of the
dragon-fly as he hovers an instant before he darts
there is a prismatic gleam. These wing textures are
even more delicate than the minute filaments on a
swallow's quill, more delicate than the pollen of a
flower. They are formed of matter indeed, but how
exquisitely it is resolved into the means and organs of
life ! Though not often consciously recognized, perhaps
this is the great pleasure of summer, to watch the
earth, the dead particles, resolving themselves into
the living case of life, to see the seed-leaf push aside
the clod and become by degrees the perfumed flower.
From the tiny mottled egg come the wings that by-
and-by shall pass the immense sea. It is in this mar-
vellous transformation of clods and cold matter into
living things that the joy and the hope of summer
reside. Every blade of grass, each leaf, each separate
floret and petal, is an inscription speaking of hope.
Consider the grasses and the oaks, the swallows, the
sweet blue butterfly—they are one and all a sign and
token showing before our eyes earth made into life.
So that my hope becomes as broad as the horizon afar,
reiterated by every leaf, sung on every bough, reflected
in the gleam of every flower. There is so much for
us yet to come, so much to be gathered, and enjoyed.
Not for you or me, now, but for our race, who will
ultimately use this magical secret for their happiness.
Earth holds secrets enough to give them the life of
the fabled Immortals. My heart is fixed firm and
stable in the belief that ultimately the sunshine and

the summer, the flowers and the azure sky, shall
become, as it were, interwoven into man's existence.
He shall take from all their beauty and enjoy their
glory. Hence it is that a flower is to me so much
more than stalk and petals. When I look in the glass
I see that every line in my face means pessimism; but
in spite of my face—that is my experience—I remain
an optimist. Time with an unsteady hand has etched
thin crooked lines, and, deepening the hollows, has cast
the original expression into shadow. Pain and sorrow
flow over us with little ceasing, as the sea-hoofs beat
on the beach. Let us not look at ourselves but onwards,
and take strength from the leaf and the signs of the
field. He is indeed despicable who cannot look onwards to the ideal life of man. Not to do so is to deny
our birthright of mind.

The long grass flowing towards the hedge has reared
in a wave against it. Along the hedge it is higher
and greener, and rustles into the very bushes. There
is a mark only now where the footpath was; it passed
close to the hedge, but its place is traceable only as a
groove in the sorrel and seed-tops. Though it has quite
filled the path, the grass there cannot send its tops so
high; it has left a winding crease. By the hedge here
stands a moss-grown willow, and its slender branches
extend over the sward. Beyond it is an oak, just
apart from the bushes; then the ground gently rises,
and an ancient pollard ash, hollow and black inside,
guards an open gateway like a low tower. The
different tone of green shows that the hedge is there
of nut-trees; but one great hawthorn spreads out in a
semicircle, roofing the grass which is yet more verdant

in the still pool (as it were) under it. Next a corner,
more oaks, and a chestnut in bloom. Returning to
this spot an old apple tree stands right out in the
meadow like an island. There seemed just now the
tiniest twinkle of movement by the rushes, but it was
lost among the hedge parsley. Among the grey leaves
of the willow there is another flit of motion; and
visible now against the sky there is a little brown
bird, not to be distinguished at the moment from the
many other little brown birds that are known to be
about. He got up into the willow from the hedge
parsley somehow, without being seen to climb or fly.
Suddenly he crosses to the tops of the hawthorn and
immediately flings himself up into the air a yard or
two, his wings and ruffled crest making a ragged outline; jerk, jerk, jerk, as if it were with the utmost
difficulty he could keep even at that height. He scolds,
and twitters, and chirps, and all at once sinks like a
stone into the hedge and out of sight as a stone into
a pond. It is a whitethroat; his nest is deep in the
parsley and nettles. Presently he will go out to the
island apple tree and back again in a minute or two;
the pair of them are so fond of each other's affectionate
company they cannot remain apart.

Watching the line of the hedge, about every two
minutes, either near at hand or yonder a bird darts
out just at the level of the grass, hovers a second with
labouring wings, and returns as swiftly to the cover.
Sometimes it is a flycatcher, sometimes a greenfinch,
or chaffinch, now and then a robin, in one place a
shrike, perhaps another is a redstart. They are fly-
fishing all of them, seizing insects from the sorrel tips

and grass, as the kingfisher takes a roach from the
water. A blackbird slips up into the oak and a dove
descends in the corner by the chestnut tree. But
these are not visible together, only one at a time and
with intervals. The larger part of the life of the
hedge is out of sight. All the thrush-fledglings, the
young blackbirds, and finches are hidden, most of
them on the mound among the ivy, and parsley, and
rough grasses, protected too by a roof of brambles.
The nests that still have eggs are not, like the nests
of the early days of April, easily found; they are deep
down in the tangled herbage by the shore of the
ditch, or far inside the thorny thickets which then
looked mere bushes, and are now so broad. Landrails
are running in the grass concealed as a man would be
in a wood; they have nests and eggs on the ground for
which you may search in vain till the mowers come.

Up in the corner a fragment of white fur and
marks of scratching show where a doe has been pre-
paring for a litter. Some well-trodden runs lead from
mound to mound; they are sandy near the hedge
where the particles have been carried out adhering to
the rabbits' feet and fur. A crow rises lazily from
the upper end of the field, and perches in the chestnut.
His presence, too, was unsuspected. He is there by
far too frequently. At this season the crows are
always in the mowing-grass, searching about, stalking
in winding tracks from furrow to furrow, picking up
an egg here and a foolish fledgling that has wandered
from the mound yonder. Very likely there may be
a moorhen or two slipping about under cover of the
long grass; thus hidden, they can leave the shelter of

the flags and wander a distance from the brook. So that beneath the surface of the grass and under the screen of the leaves there are ten times more birds than are seen.

Besides the singing and calling, there is a peculiar sound which is only heard in summer. Waiting quietly to discover what birds are about, I become aware of a sound in the very air. It is not the mid-summer hum which will soon be heard over the heated hay in the valley and over the cooler hills alike. It is not enough to be called a hum, and does but just tremble at the extreme edge of hearing. If the branches wave and rustle they overbear it; the buzz of a passing bee is so much louder it overcomes all of it that is in the whole field. I cannot define it, except by calling the hours of winter to mind—they are silent; you hear a branch crack or creak as it rubs another in the wood, you hear the hoar frost crunch on the grass beneath your feet, but the air is without sound in itself. The sound of summer is everywhere —in the passing breeze, in the hedge, in the broad-branching trees, in the grass as it swings; all the myriad particles that together make the summer are in motion. The sap moves in the trees, the pollen is pushed out from grass and flower, and yet again these acres and acres of leaves and square miles of grass blades—for they would cover acres and square miles if reckoned edge to edge—are drawing their strength from the atmosphere. Exceedingly minute as these vibrations must be, their numbers perhaps may give them a volume almost reaching in the aggre-gate to the power of the ear. Besides the quivering

leaf, the swinging grass, the fluttering bird's wing,
and the thousand oval membranes which innumerable
insects whirl about, a faint resonance seems to come
from the very earth itself. The fervour of the sunbeams descending in a tidal flood rings on the strung
harp of earth. It is this exquisite undertone, heard
and yet unheard, which brings the mind into sweet
accordance with the wonderful instrument of nature.

By the apple tree there is a low bank, where the
grass is less tall and admits the heat direct to the
ground; here there are blue flowers — bluer than
the wings of my favourite butterflies—with white
centres — the lovely bird's-eyes, or veronica. The
violet and cowslip, bluebell and rose, are known to
thousands; the veronica is overlooked. The ploughboys know it, and the wayside children, the mower
and those who linger in fields, but few else. Brightly
blue and surrounded by greenest grass, imbedded in
and all the more blue for the shadow of the grass,
these growing butterflies' wings draw to themselves
the sun. From this island I look down into the depth
of the grasses. Red sorrel spires—deep drinkers of
reddest sun wine—stand the boldest, and in their
numbers threaten the buttercups. To these in the
distance they give the gipsy-gold tint—the reflection
of fire on plates of the precious metal. It will show
even on a ring by firelight; blood in the gold, they
say. Gather the open marguerite daisies, and they
seem large—so wide a disc, such fingers of rays; but
in the grass their size is toned by so much green.
Clover heads of honey lurk in the bunches and by the
hidden footpath. Like clubs from Polynesia the tips

E

of the grasses are varied in shape: some tend to a point—the foxtails—some are hard and cylindrical; others, avoiding the club shape, put forth the slenderest branches with fruit of seed at the ends, which tremble as the air goes by. Their stalks are ripening and becoming of the colour of hay while yet the long blades remain green.

Each kind is repeated a hundred times, the foxtails are succeeded by foxtails, the narrow blades by narrow blades, but never become monotonous; sorrel stands by sorrel, daisy flowers by daisy. This bed of veronica at the foot of the ancient apple has a whole handful of flowers, and yet they do not weary the eye. Oak follows oak and elm ranks with elm, but the woodlands are pleasant; however many times reduplicated, their beauty only increases. So, too, the summer days; the sun rises on the same grasses and green hedges, there is the same blue sky, but did we ever have enough of them? No, not in a hundred years! There seems always a depth, somewhere, unexplored, a thicket that has not been seen through, a corner full of ferns, a quaint old hollow tree, which may give us something. Bees go by me as I stand under the apple, but they pass on for the most part bound on a long journey, across to the clover fields or up to the thyme lands; only a few go down into the mowing-grass. The hive bees are the most impatient of insects; they cannot bear to entangle their wings beating against grasses or boughs. Not one will enter a hedge. They like an open and level surface, places cropped by sheep, the sward by the roadside, fields of clover, where the flower is not deep under grass.

II.

It is the patient humble-bee that goes down into the forest of the mowing-grass. If entangled, the humble-bee climbs up a sorrel stem and takes wing, without any sign of annoyance. His broad back with tawny bar buoyantly glides over the golden butter-cups. He hums to himself as he goes, so happy is he. He knows no skep, no cunning work in glass receives his labour, no artificial saccharine aids him when the beams of the sun are cold, there is no step to his house that he may alight in comfort; the way is not made clear for him that he may start straight for the flowers, nor are any sown for him. He has no shelter if the storm descends suddenly; he has no dome of twisted straw well thatched and tiled to retreat to. The butcher-bird, with a beak like a crooked iron nail, drives him to the ground, and leaves him pierced with a thorn; but no hail of shot revenges his tortures. The grass stiffens at nightfall (in autumn), and he must creep where he may, if possibly he may escape the frost. No one cares for the humble-bee. But down to the flowering nettle in the mossy-sided ditch, up into the tall elm, winding in and out and round the branched buttercups, along the banks of the brook, far inside the deepest wood, away he wanders and despises nothing. His nest is under the rough grasses and the mosses of the mound, a mere tunnel beneath the fibres and matted surface. The hawthorn over-hangs it, the fern grows by, red mice rustle past.

It thunders, and the great oak trembles; the heavy rain drops through the treble roof of oak and hawthorn and fern. Under the arched branches the lightning plays along, swiftly to and fro, or seems to, like the swish of a whip, a yellowish-red against the green; a boom! a crackle as if a tree fell from the sky. The thick grasses are bowed, the white florets of the wild parsley are beaten down, the rain hurls itself, and suddenly a fierce blast tears the green oak leaves and whirls them out into the fields; but the humble-bee's home, under moss and matted fibres, remains uninjured. His house at the root of the king of trees, like a cave in the rock, is safe. The storm passes and the sun comes out, the air is the sweeter and the richer for the rain, like verses with a rhyme; there will be more honey in the flowers. Humble he is, but wild; always in the field, the wood; always by the banks and thickets; always wild and humming to his flowers. Therefore I like the humble-bee, being, at heart at least, for ever roaming among the woodlands and the hills and by the brooks. In such quick summer storms the lightning gives the impression of being far more dangerous than the zigzag paths traced on the autumn sky. The electric cloud seems almost level with the ground and the livid flame to rush to and fro beneath the boughs as the little bats do in the evening.

Caught by such a cloud, I have stayed under thick larches at the edge of plantations. They are no shelter, but conceal one perfectly. The wood pigeons come home to their nest trees; in larches they seem to have permanent nests, almost like rooks. Kestrels, too, come home to the wood. Pheasants crow, but not from fear—from defiance; in fear they scream. The

boom startles them, and they instantly defy the sky.
The rabbits quietly feed on out in the field between
the thistles and rushes that so often grow in woodside
pastures, quietly hopping to their favourite places,
utterly heedless how heavy the echoes may be in the
hollows of the wooded hills. Till the rain comes they
take no heed whatever, but then make for shelter.
Blackbirds often make a good deal of noise; but the
soft turtle-doves coo gently, let the lightning be as
savage as it will. Nothing has the least fear. Man
alone, more senseless than a pigeon, put a god in
vapour; and to this day, though the printing press has
set a foot on every threshold, numbers bow the knee
when they hear the roar the timid dove does not heed.
So trustful are the doves, the squirrels, the birds of the
branches, and the creatures of the field. Under their
tuition let us rid ourselves of mental terrors, and face
death itself as calmly as they do the livid lightning;
so trustful and so content with their fate, resting in
themselves and unappalled. If but by reason and will
I could reach the godlike calm and courage of what we
so thoughtlessly call the timid turtle-dove, I should
lead a nearly perfect life.

The bark of the ancient apple tree under which I
have been standing is shrunken like iron which has
been heated and let cool round the rim of a wheel.
For a hundred years the horses have rubbed against it
while feeding in the aftermath. The scales of the bark
are gone or smoothed down and level, so that insects
have no hiding-place. There are no crevices for them,
the horsehairs that were caught anywhere have been
carried away by birds for their nests. The trunk is

smooth and columnar, hard as iron. A hundred times
the mowing-grass has grown up around it, the birds
have built their nests, the butterflies fluttered by, and
the acorns dropped from the oaks. It is a long, long
time, counted by artificial hours or by the seasons, but
it is longer still in another way. The greenfinch in
the hawthorn yonder has been there since I came out,
and all the time has been happily talking to his love.
He has left the hawthorn indeed, but only for a
minute or two, to fetch a few seeds, and comes back
each time more full of song-talk than ever. He notes
no slow movement of the oak's shadow on the grass;
it is nothing to him and his lady dear that the sun, as
seen from his nest, is crossing from one great bough of
the oak to another. The dew even in the deepest and
most tangled grass has long since been dried, and some
of the flowers that close at noon will shortly fold their
petals. The morning airs, which breathe so sweetly,
come less and less frequently as the heat increases.
Vanishing from the sky, the last fragments of cloud
have left an untarnished azure. Many times the bees
have returned to their hives, and thus the index of the
day advances. It is nothing to the greenfinches; all
their thoughts are in their song-talk. The sunny
moment is to them all in all. So deeply are they rapt
in it that they do not know whether it is a moment or
a year. There is no clock for feeling, for joy, for love.

And with all their motions and stepping from bough
to bough, they are not restless; they have so much
time, you see. So, too, the whitethroat in the wild
parsley; so, too, the thrush that just now peered out
and partly fluttered his wings as he stood to look. A

butterfly comes and stays on a leaf—a leaf much
warmed by the sun—and shuts his wings. In a
minute he opens them, shuts them again, half wheels
round, and by-and-by—just when he chooses, and not
before—floats away. The flowers open, and remain
open for hours, to the sun. Hastelessness is the only
word one can make up to describe it; there is much
rest, but no haste. Each moment, as with the greenfinches, is so full of life that it seems so long and so
sufficient in itself. Not only the days, but life itself
lengthens in summer. I would spread abroad my arms
and gather more of it to me, could I do so.

All the procession of living and growing things
passes. The grass stands up taller and still taller, the
sheaths open, and the stalk arises, the pollen clings till
the breeze sweeps it. The bees rush past, and the
resolute wasps; the humble-bees, whose weight swings
them along. About the oaks and maples the brown
chafers swarm, and the fern-owls at dusk, and the
blackbirds and jays by day, cannot reduce their legions
while they last. Yellow butterflies, and white, broad
red admirals, and sweet blues; think of the kingdom
of flowers which is theirs! Heavy moths burring at
the edge of the copse; green, and red, and gold flies:
gnats, like smoke, around the tree-tops; midges so
thick over the brook, as if you could haul a netful;
tiny leaping creatures in the grass; bronze beetles
across the path; blue dragonflies pondering on cool
leaves of water-plantain. Blue jays flitting, a magpie
drooping across from elm to elm; young rooks that
have escaped the hostile shot blundering up into the
branches; missel thrushes leading their fledglings,

already strong on the wing, from field to field. An egg here on the sward dropped by a starling; a red ladybird creeping, tortoise-like, up a green fern frond. Finches undulating through the air, shooting themselves with closed wings, and linnets happy with their young.

Golden dandelion discs—gold and orange—of a hue more beautiful, I think, than the higher and more visible buttercup. A blackbird, gleaming, so black is he, splashing in the runlet of water across the gateway. A ruddy kingfisher swiftly drawing himself, as you might draw a stroke with a pencil, over the surface of the yellow buttercups, and away above the hedge. Hart's-tongue fern, thick with green, so green as to be thick with its colour, deep in the ditch under the shady hazel boughs. White meadow-sweet lifting its tiny florets, and black-flowered sedges. You must push through the reed grass to find the sword-flags; the stout willow-herbs will not be trampled down, but resist the foot like underwood. Pink lychnis flowers behind the withy stoles, and little black moorhens swim away, as you gather it, after their mother, who has dived under the water-grass, and broken the smooth surface of the duckweed. Yellow loosestrife is rising, thick comfrey stands at the very edge; the sandpipers run where the shore is free from bushes. Back by the underwood the prickly and repellent brambles will presently present us with fruit. For the squirrels the nuts are forming, green beechmast is there —green wedges under the spray; up in the oaks the small knots, like bark rolled up in a dot, will be acorns. Purple vetches along the mounds, yellow lotus where

the grass is shorter, and orchis succeeds to orchis. As
I write them, so these things come—not set in grada-
tion, but like the broadcast flowers in the mowing-
grass.

Now follows the gorse, and the pink rest-harrow,
and the sweet lady's-bedstraw, set as it were in the
midst of a little thorn-bush. The broad repetition of
the yellow clover is not to be written; acre upon acre,
and not one spot of green, as if all the green had been
planed away, leaving only the flowers to which the
bees come by the thousand from far and near. But
one white campion stands in the midst of the lake of
yellow. The field is scented as though a hundred
hives of honey had been emptied on it. Along the
mound by it the bluebells are seeding, the hedge has
been cut and the ground is strewn with twigs. Among
those seeding bluebells and dry twigs and mosses I
think a titlark has his nest, as he stays all day there
and in the oak over. The pale clear yellow of charlock, sharp and clear, promises the finches bushels of
seed for their young. Under the scarlet of the poppies
the larks run, and then for change of colour soar into
the blue. Creamy honeysuckle on the hedge around
the cornfield, buds of wild rose everywhere, but no
sweet petal yet. Yonder, where the wheat can climb
no higher up the slope, are the purple heath-bells,
thyme and flitting stonechats.

The lone barn shut off by acres of barley is noisy
with sparrows. It is their city, and there is a nest in
every crevice, almost under every tile. Sometimes the
partridges run between the ricks, and when the bats
come out of the roof, leverets play in the waggon-track.

At even a fern-owl beats by, passing close to the eaves
whence the moths issue. On the narrow waggon-
track which descends along a coombe and is worn in
chalk, the heat pours down by day as if an invisible
lens in the atmosphere focussed the sun's rays. Strong
woody knapweed endures it, so does toadflax and pale
blue scabious, and wild mignonette. The very sun of
Spain burns and burns and ripens the wheat on the
edge of the coombe, and will only let the spring
moisten a yard or two around it; but there a few
rushes have sprung, and in the water itself brooklime
with blue flowers grows so thickly that nothing but a
bird could find space to drink. So down again from
this sun of Spain to woody coverts where the wild
hops are blocking every avenue, and green-flowered
bryony would fain climb to the trees; where grey-flecked
ivy winds spirally about the red rugged bark of pines,
where burdocks fight for the footpath, and teazle-heads
look over the low hedges. Brake-fern rises five feet
high; in some way woodpeckers are associated with
brake, and there seem more of them where it flourishes.
If you count the depth and strength of its roots in the
loamy sand, add the thickness of its flattened stem,
and the width of its branching fronds, you may say
that it comes near to be a little tree. Beneath where
the ponds are bushy mare's-tails grow, and on the
moist banks jointed pewterwort; some of the broad
bronze leaves of water-weeds seem to try and conquer
the pond and cover it so firmly that a wagtail may
run on them. A white butterfly follows along the
waggon-road, the pheasants slip away as quietly as the
butterfly flies, but a jay screeches loudly and flutters

in high rage to see us. Under an ancient garden wall
among matted bines of trumpet convolvulus, there is a
hedge-sparrow's nest overhung with ivy on which
even now the last black berries cling.

There are minute white flowers on the top of the
wall, out of reach, and lichen grows against it dried by
the sun till it looks ready to crumble. By the gateway grows a thick bunch of meadow geranium, soon
to flower; over the gate is the dusty highway road,
quiet but dusty, dotted with the innumerable foot-
marks of a flock of sheep that has passed. The sound
of their bleating still comes back, and the bees driven
up by their feet have hardly had time to settle again
on the white clover beginning to flower on the short
roadside sward. All the hawthorn leaves and briar
and bramble, the honeysuckle, too, is gritty with the
dust that has been scattered upon it. But see—can it
be ? Stretch a hand high, quick, and reach it down;
the first, the sweetest, the dearest rose of June. Not
yet expected, for the time is between the may and the
roses, least of all here in the hot and dusty highway;
but it is found—the first rose of June.

Straight go the white petals to the heart; straight
the mind's glance goes back to how many other
pageants of summer in old times ! When perchance
the sunny days were even more sunny; when the
stilly oaks were full of mystery, lurking like the
Druid's mistletoe in the midst of their mighty branches.
A glamour in the heart came back to it again from
every flower; as the sunshine was reflected from them
so the feeling in the heart returned tenfold. To the
dreamy summer haze love gave a deep enchantment,

the colours were fairer, the blue more lovely in the lucid sky. Each leaf finer, and the gross earth enamelled beneath the feet. A sweet breath on the air, a soft warm hand in the touch of the sunshine, a glance in the gleam of the rippled waters, a whisper in the dance of the shadows. The ethereal haze lifted the heavy oaks and they were buoyant on the mead, the rugged bark was chastened and no longer rough, each slender flower beneath them again refined. There was a presence everywhere though unseen, on the open hills, and not shut out under the dark pines. Dear were the June roses then because for another gathered. Yet even dearer now with so many years as it were upon the petals; all the days that have been before, all the heart-throbs, all our hopes lie in this opened bud. Let not the eyes grow dim, look not back but forward ; the soul must uphold itself like the sun. Let us labour to make the heart grow larger as we become older, as the spreading oak gives more shelter. That we could but take to the soul some of the greatness and the beauty of the summer !

Still the pageant moves. The song-talk of the finches rises and sinks like the tinkle of a waterfall. The greenfinches have been by me all the while. A bullfinch pipes now and then further up the hedge where the brambles and thorns are thickest. Boldest of birds to look at, he is always in hiding. The shrill tone of a goldfinch came just now from the ash branches, but he has gone on. Every four or five minutes a chaffinch sings close by, and another fills the interval near the gateway. There are linnets somewhere, but I cannot from the old apple tree fix their exact place. Thrushes have sung and ceased; they will begin again in ten minutes. The blackbirds do not cease; the note uttered by a blackbird in the oak yonder before it can drop is taken up by a second near the top of the field, and ere it falls is caught by a third on the left-hand side. From one of the topmost boughs of an elm there fell the song of a willow warbler for awhile; one of the least of birds, he often seeks the highest branches of the highest tree.

A yellowhammer has just flown from a bare branch in the gateway, where he has been perched and singing a full hour. Presently he will commence again, and as the sun declines will sing him to the horizon, and then again sing till nearly dusk. The yellowhammer is almost the longest of all the singers; he sits and sits and has no inclination to move. In the spring he sings, in the summer he sings, and he continues when the last sheaves are being carried from the wheat field. The redstart yonder has given forth a few notes, the whitethroat flings himself into the air at short intervals and chatters, the shrike calls sharp and determined, faint but shrill calls descend from the swifts in the air. These descend, but the twittering notes of the swallows do not reach so far—they are too high to-day. A cuckoo has called by the brook, and now fainter from a greater distance. That the titlarks are singing I know, but not within hearing from here; a dove, though, is audible, and a chiffchaff has twice passed. Afar beyond the oaks at the top of the field dark specks ascend from time to time, and after moving in wide circles for awhile descend again to the corn. These must be larks; but their notes are not powerful

enough to reach me, though they would were it not
for the song in the hedges, the hum of innumerable
insects, and the ceaseless " crake, crake " of landrails.
There are at least two landrails in the mowing-grass ;
one of them just now seemed coming straight towards
the apple tree, and I expected in a minute to see the
grass move, when the bird turned aside and entered
the tufts and wild parsley by the hedge.   Thence the
call has come without a moment's pause, " crake, crake,"
till the thick hedge seems filled with it.   Tits have
visited the apple tree over my head, a wren has sung
in the willow, or rather on a dead branch projecting
lower down than the leafy boughs, and a robin across
under the elms in the opposite hedge.   Elms are a
favourite tree of robins—not the upper branches, but
those that grow down the trunk, and are the first to
have leaves in spring.

The yellowhammer is the most persistent indi-
vidually, but I think the blackbirds when listened
to are the masters of the fields.   Before one can
finish another begins, like the summer ripples succeed-
ing behind each other, so that the melodious sound
merely changes its position.   Now here, now in the
corner, then across the field, again in the distant
copse, where it seems about to sink, when it rises again
almost at hand.   Like a great human artist, the blackbird makes no effort, being fully conscious that his
liquid tone cannot be matched.   He utters a few delicious notes, and carelessly quits the green stage of the
oak till it pleases him to sing again.   Without the
blackbird, in whose throat the sweetness of the green
fields dwells, the days would be only partly summer.

Without the violet all the bluebells and cowslips could
not make a spring, and without the blackbird, even
the nightingale would be but half welcome. It is not
yet noon, these songs have been ceaseless since dawn;
this evening, after the yellowhammer has sung the sun
down, when the moon rises and the faint stars appear,
still the cuckoo will call, and the grasshopper lark, the
landrail's "crake, crake" will echo from the mound, a
warbler or a blackcap will utter his notes, and even at
the darkest of the summer night the swallows will
hardly sleep in their nests. As the morning sky grows
blue, an hour before the sun, up will rise the larks
singing and audible now, the cuckoo will recommence,
and the swallows will start again on their tireless
journey. So that the songs of the summer birds are
as ceaseless as the sound of the waterfall which plays
day and night.

I cannot leave it; I must stay under the old tree in
the midst of the long grass, the luxury of the leaves,
and the song in the very air. I seem as if I could
feel all the glowing life the sunshine gives and the
south wind calls to being. The endless grass, the endless leaves, the immense strength of the oak expanding,
the unalloyed joy of finch and blackbird; from all of
them I receive a little. Each gives me something of
the pure joy they gather for themselves. In the
blackbird's melody one note is mine; in the dance of
the leaf shadows the formed maze is for me, though
the motion is theirs; the flowers with a thousand faces
have collected the kisses of the morning. Feeling with
them, I receive some, at least, of their fulness of life.
Never could I have enough; never stay long enough—

whether here or whether lying on the shorter sward under the sweeping and graceful birches, or on the thyme-scented hills. Hour after hour, and still not enough. Or walking the footpath was never long enough, or my strength sufficient to endure till the mind was weary. The exceeding beauty of the earth, in her splendour of life, yields a new thought with every petal. The hours when the mind is absorbed by beauty are the only hours when we really live, so that the longer we can stay among these things so much the more is snatched from inevitable Time. Let the shadow advance upon the dial—I can watch it with equanimity while it is there to be watched. It is only when the shadow is *not* there, when the clouds of winter cover it, that the dial is terrible. The invisible shadow goes on and steals from us. But now, while I can see the shadow of the tree and watch it slowly gliding along the surface of the grass, it is mine. These are the only hours that are not wasted—these hours that absorb the soul and fill it with beauty. This is real life, and all else is illusion, or mere endurance. Does this reverie of flowers and waterfall and song form an ideal, a human ideal, in the mind? It does; much the same ideal that Phidias sculptured of man and woman filled with a godlike sense of the violet fields of Greece, beautiful beyond thought, calm as my turtle-dove before the lurid lightning of the unknown. To be beautiful and to be calm, without mental fear, is the ideal of nature. If I cannot achieve it, at least I can think it.

MEADOW THOUGHTS.

THE old house stood by the silent country road, secluded by many a long, long mile, and yet again secluded within the great walls of the garden. Often and often I rambled up to the milestone which stood under an oak, to look at the chipped inscription low down—" To London, 79 Miles." So far away, you see, that the very inscription was cut at the foot of the stone, since no one would be likely to want that information. It was half hidden by docks and nettles, despised and unnoticed. A broad land this seventy-nine miles—how many meadows and corn-fields, hedges and woods, in that distance ?—wide enough to seclude any house, to hide it, like an acorn in the grass. Those who have lived all their lives in remote places do not feel the remoteness. No one else seemed to be conscious of the breadth that separated the place from the great centre, but it was, perhaps, that consciousness which deepened the solitude to me. It made the silence more still ; the shadows of the oaks yet slower in their movement ; everything more earnest. To convey a full impression of the intense concentration of Nature in the meadows is very difficult—everything

F

is so utterly oblivious of man's thought and man's heart. The oaks stand—quiet, still—so still that the lichen loves them. At their feet the grass grows, and heeds nothing. Among it the squirrels leap, and their little hearts are as far away from you or I as the very wood of the oaks. The sunshine settles itself in the valley by the brook, and abides there whether we come or not. Glance through the gap in the hedge by the oak, and see how concentrated it is—all of it, every blade of grass, and leaf, and flower, and living creature, finch or squirrel. It is mesmerised upon itself. Then I used to feel that it really was seventy-nine miles to London, and not an hour or two only by rail, really all those miles. A great, broad province of green furrow and ploughed furrow between the old house and the city of the world. Such solace and solitude seventy-nine miles thick cannot be painted; the trees cannot be placed far enough away in perspective. It is necessary to stay in it like the oaks to know it.

Lime-tree branches overhung the corner of the garden-wall, whence a view was easy of the silent and dusty road, till overarching oaks concealed it. The white dust heated by the sunshine, the green hedges, and the heavily massed trees, white clouds rolled together in the sky, a footpath opposite lost in the fields, as you might thrust a stick into the grass, tender lime leaves caressing the cheek, and silence. That is, the silence of the fields. If a breeze rustled the boughs, if a greenfinch called, if the cart-mare in the meadow shook herself, making the earth and air tremble by her with the convulsion of her mighty muscles, these were not sounds, they were the silence itself. So sensitive to it as I was, in its turn it held me firmly, like the fabled spells of old time. The mere touch of a leaf was a talisman to bring me under the enchantment, so that I seemed to feel and know all that was proceeding among the grass-blades and in the bushes. Among the lime trees along the wall the birds never built, though so close and sheltered. They built everywhere but there. To the broad coping-stones of the wall under the lime boughs speckled thrushes came almost hourly, sometimes to peer out and reconnoitre if it was safe to visit the garden, sometimes to see if a snail had climbed up the ivy. Then they dropped quietly down into the long strawberry patch immediately under. The cover of strawberries is the constant resource of all creeping things; the thrushes looked round every plant and under every leaf and runner. One toad always resided there, often two, and as you gathered a ripe strawberry you might catch sight of his black eye watching you take the fruit he had saved for you.

Down the road skims an eave-swallow, swift as an arrow, his white back making the sun-dried dust dull and dingy; he is seeking a pool for mortar, and will waver to and fro by the brook below till he finds a convenient place to alight. Thence back to the eave here, where for forty years he and his ancestors built in safety. Two white butterflies fluttering round each other rise over the limes, once more up over the house, and soar on till their white shows no longer against the illumined air. A grasshopper calls on the sward by the strawberries, and immediately fillips

himself over seven leagues of grass-blades. Yonder
a line of men and women file across the field, seen for
a moment as they pass a gateway, and the hay changes
from hay-colour to green behind them as they turn
the under but still sappy side upwards. They are
working hard, but it looks easy, slow, and sunny.
Finches fly out from the hedgerow to the overturned
hay. Another butterfly, a brown one, floats along the
dusty road—the only traveller yet. The white clouds
are slowly passing behind the oaks, large puffed clouds,
like deliberate loads of hay, leaving little wisps and
flecks behind them caught in the sky. How pleasant
it would be to read in the shadow ! There is a broad
shadow on the sward by the strawberries cast by
a tall and fine-grown American crab tree. The very
place for a book ; and although I know it is useless,
yet I go and fetch one and dispose myself on the grass.

I can never read in summer out-of-doors. Though
in shadow the bright light fills it, summer shadows are
broadest daylight. The page is so white and hard, the
letters so very black, the meaning and drift not quite
intelligible, because neither eye nor mind will dwell
upon it. Human thoughts and imaginings written
down are pale and feeble in bright summer light. The
eye wanders away, and rests more lovingly on greensward and green lime leaves. The mind wanders yet
deeper and farther into the dreamy mystery of the azure
sky. Once now and then, determined to write down
that mystery and delicious sense while actually in it, I
have brought out table and ink and paper, and sat there
in the midst of the summer day. Three words, and
where is the thought ? Gone. The paper is so obviously

paper, the ink so evidently ink, the pen so stiff; all so inadequate. You want colour, flexibility, light, sweet low sound—all these to paint it and play it in music, at the same time you want something that will answer to and record in one touch the strong throb of life and the thought, or feeling, or whatever it is that goes out into the earth and sky and space, endless as a beam of light. The very shade of the pen on the paper tells you how utterly hopeless it is to express these things. There is the shade and the brilliant gleaming whiteness; now tell me in plain written words the simple contrast of the two. Not in twenty pages, for the bright light shows the paper in its common fibre-ground, coarse aspect, in its reality, not as a mind-tablet.

The delicacy and beauty of thought or feeling is so extreme that it cannot be inked in; it is like the green and blue of field and sky, of veronica flower and grass blade, which in their own existence throw light and beauty on each other, but in artificial colours repel. Take the table indoors again, and the book; the thoughts and imaginings of others are vain, and of your own too deep to be written. For the mind is filled with the exceeding beauty of these things, and their great wondrousness and marvel. Never yet have I been able to write what I felt about the sunlight only. Colour and form and light are as magic to me. It is a trance. It requires a language of ideas to convey it. It is ten years since I last reclined on that grass plot, and yet I have been writing of it as if it was yesterday, and every blade of grass is as visible and as real to me now as then. They were greener towards the house, and more brown-tinted on the margin of the strawberry bed, because towards the house the shadow rested longest. By the strawberries the fierce sunlight burned them.

The sunlight put out the books I brought into it just as it put out the fire on the hearth indoors. The tawny flames floating upwards could not bite the crackling sticks when the full beams came pouring on them. Such extravagance of light overcame the little fire till it was screened from the power of the heavens. So here in the shadow of the American crab tree the light of the sky put out the written pages. For this beautiful and wonderful light excited a sense of some likewise beautiful and wonderful truth, some unknown but grand thought hovering as a swallow above. The swallows hovered and did not alight, but they were there. An inexpressible thought quivered in the azure overhead ; it could not be fully grasped, but there was a sense and feeling of its presence. Before that mere sense of its presence the weak and feeble pages, the small fires of human knowledge, dwindled and lost meaning. There was something here that was not in the books. In all the philosophies and searches of mind there was nothing that could be brought to face it, to say, This is what it intends, this is the explanation of the dream. The very grass-blades confounded the wisest, the tender lime leaf put them to shame, the grasshopper derided them, the sparrow on the wall chirped his scorn. The books were put out, unless a screen were placed between them and the light of the sky—that is, an assumption, so as to make an artificial mental darkness. Grant some assumptions—that is, screen off the light—and in that darkness everything was easily arranged, this thing here, and that yonder. But nature grants no assumptions, and the books were put out. There is something beyond the philosophies in the light, in the grass-blades, the leaf, the grass-hopper, the sparrow on the wall. Some day the great and beautiful thought which hovers on the confines of the mind will at last alight. In that is hope, the whole sky is full of abounding hope. Something beyond the books, that is consolation.

The little lawn beside the strawberry bed, burned brown there, and green towards the house shadow, holds how many myriad grass-blades ? Here they are all matted together, long, and dragging each other down. Part them, and beneath them are still more, overhung and hidden. The fibres are intertangled, woven in an endless basket-work and chaos of green and dried threads. A blamable profusion this ; a fifth as many would be enough ; altogether a wilful waste here. As for these insects that spring out of it as I press the grass, a hundredth part of them would suffice. The American crab tree is a snowy mount in spring ; the flakes of bloom, when they fall, cover the grass with a film—a bushel of bloom, which the wind takes and scatters afar. The extravagance is sublime. The two little cherry trees are as wasteful ; they throw away handfuls of flower ; but in the meadows the careless, spendthrift ways of grass and flower and all things are not to be expressed. Seeds by the hundred million float with absolute indifference on the air. The oak has a hundred thousand more leaves than necessary, and never hides a single acorn. Nothing utilitarian—everything on a scale of splendid waste. Such noble, broadcast, open-armed waste is delicious to behold. Never was there such a lying proverb as " Enough is as good as a feast." Give me the feast ; give me squandered millions of seeds, luxurious carpets of petals, green mountains of oak leaves. The greater the waste, the greater the enjoyment—the nearer the approach to real life. Casuistry is of no avail; the fact is obvious ; Nature flings treasures abroad, puffs them with open lips along on every breeze, piles up lavish layers of them in the free open air, packs countless numbers together in the needles of a fir tree. Prodigality and superfluity are stamped on everything she does. The ear of wheat returns a hundredfold the grain from which it grew. The surface of the earth offers to us far more than we can consume—the grains, the seeds, the fruits, the animals, the abounding products are beyond the power of all the human race to devour. They can, too, be multiplied a thousandfold. There is no natural lack. Whenever there is lack among us it is from artificial causes, which intelligence should remove.

From the littleness, and meanness, and niggardliness forced upon us by circumstances, what a relief to turn aside to the exceeding plenty of Nature ! There are no bounds to it, there is no comparison to parallel it, so great is this generosity. No physical reason exists why every human being should not have sufficient, at least, of necessities. For any human being to starve, or even to be in trouble about the procuring of simple food, appears, indeed, a strange and unaccountable thing, quite upside down, and contrary to sense, if you do but consider a moment the enormous profusion the earth throws at our feet. In the slow process of time, as the human heart grows larger, such provision, I sincerely trust, will be made that no one need ever feel anxiety about mere subsistence. Then, too, let there be some imitation of this open-handed generosity and divine waste. Let the generations to come feast free of care, like my finches on the seeds of the mowing-grass, from which no voice drives them. If I could but give away as freely as the earth does !

The white-backed eave-swallow has returned many, many times from the shallow drinking-place by the brook to his half-built nest. Sometimes the pair of them cling to the mortar they have fixed under the eave, and twitter to each other about the progress of the work. They dive downwards with such velocity when they quit hold that it seems as if they must strike the ground, but they shoot up again, over the wall and the lime trees. A thrush has been to the arbour yonder twenty times ; it is made of crossed laths, and overgrown with " tea-plant," and the nest is inside the lathwork. A sparrow has visited the rose tree by the wall—the buds are covered with aphides. A brown tree-creeper has been to the limes, then to the cherries, and even to a stout lilac stem. No matter how small the tree, he tries all that are in his way. The bright colours of a bullfinch were visible a moment just now, as he passed across the shadows farther down the garden under the damson trees and into the bushes. The grasshopper has gone past and along the garden-path, his voice is not heard now ; but there is another

coming. While I have been dreaming, all these and
hundreds out in the meadow have been intensely
happy. So concentrated on their little work in the
sunshine, so intent on the tiny egg, on the insect
captured on the grass-tip to be carried to the eager
fledglings, so joyful in listening to the song poured
out for them or in pouring it forth, quite oblivious of
all else. It is in this intense concentration that they
are so happy. If they could only live longer!—but a
few such seasons for them—I wish they could live a
hundred years just to feast on the seeds and sing and
be utterly happy and oblivious of everything but the
moment they are passing. A black line has rushed up
from the espalier apple yonder to the housetop thirty
times at least. The starlings fly so swiftly and so
straight that they seem to leave a black line along the
air. They have a nest in the roof, they are to and fro
it and the meadow the entire day, from dawn till eve.
The espalier apple, like a screen, hides the meadow
from me, so that the descending starlings appear to
dive into a space behind it. Sloping downwards the
meadow makes a valley; I cannot see it, but know
that it is golden with buttercups, and that a brook
runs in the groove of it.

Afar yonder I can see a summit beyond where the
grass swells upwards to a higher level than this spot.
There are bushes and elms whose height is decreased
by distance on the summit, horses in the shadow of the
trees, and a small flock of sheep crowded, as is their
wont, in the hot and sunny gateway. By the side of
the summit is a deep green trench, so it looks from
here, in the hill-side : it is really the course of a

streamlet worn deep in the earth. I can see nothing between the top of the espalier screen and the horses under the elms on the hill. But the starlings go up and down into the hollow space, which is aglow with golden buttercups, and, indeed, I am looking over a hundred finches eagerly searching, sweetly calling, happy as the summer day. A thousand thousand grasshoppers are leaping, thrushes are labouring, filled with love and tenderness, doves cooing—there is as much joy as there are leaves on the hedges. Faster than the starling's flight my mind runs up to the streamlet in the deep green trench beisde the hill.

Pleasant it was to trace it upwards, narrowing at every ascending step, till the thin stream, thinner than fragile glass, did but merely slip over the stones. A little less and it could not have run at all, water could not stretch out to greater tenuity. It smoothed the brown growth on the stones, stroking it softly. It filled up tiny basins of sand, and ran out at the edges between minute rocks of flint. Beneath it went under thickest brooklime, -blue flowered, and serrated water-parsnips, lost like many a mighty river for awhile among a forest of leaves. Higher up masses of bramble and projecting thorn stopped the explorer, who must wind round the grassy mound. Pausing to look back a moment there were meads under the hill with the shortest and greenest herbage, perpetually watered, and without one single buttercup, a strip of pure green among yellow flowers and yellowing corn. A few hollow oaks on whose boughs the cuckoos stayed to call, two or three peewits coursing up and down, larks singing, and for all else silence.

Between the wheat and the grassy mound the path was almost closed, burdocks and brambles thrust the adventurer outward to brush against the wheat-ears.   Upwards till suddenly it turned, and led by steep notches in the bank, as it seemed down to the roots of the elm trees.   The clump of elms grew right over a deep and rugged hollow; their branches reached out across it, roofing in the cave.

Here was the spring, at the foot of a perpendicular rock, moss-grown low down, and overrun with creeping ivy higher.   Green thorn bushes filled the chinks and made a wall to the well, and the long narrow hart's-tongue streaked the face of the cliff.   Behind the thick thorns hid the course of the streamlet, in front rose the solid rock, upon the right hand the sward came to the edge—it shook every now and then as the horses in the shade of the elms stamped their feet—on the left hand the ears of wheat peered over the verge.   A rocky cell in concentrated silence of green things.   Now and again a finch, a starling, or a sparrow would come meaning to drink—athirst from the meadow or the corn-field—and start and almost entangle their wings in the bushes, so completely astonished that any one should be there.   The spring rises in a hollow under the rock imperceptibly, and without bubble or sound.   The fine sand of the shallow basin is undisturbed—no tiny water-volcano pushes up a dome of particles.   Nor is there any crevice in the stone, but the basin is always full and always running over.   As it slips from the brim a gleam of sunshine falls through the boughs and meets it.   To this cell I used to come once now and then on a summer's day, tempted, perhaps, like the finches, by the sweet cool water, but drawn also by a feeling that could not be analysed. Stooping, I lifted the water in the hollow of my hand—carefully, lest the sand might be disturbed—and the sunlight gleamed on it as it slipped through my fingers. Alone in the green-roofed cave, alone with the sunlight and the pure water, there was a sense of something more than these. The water was more to me than water, and the sun than sun. The gleaming rays on the water in my palm held me for a moment, the touch of the water gave me something from itself. A moment, and the gleam was gone, the water flowing away, but I had had them. Beside the physical water and physical light I had received from them their beauty; they had communicated to me this silent mystery. The pure and beautiful water, the pure, clear, and beautiful light, each had given me something of their truth.

So many times I came to it, toiling up the long and shadowless hill in the burning sunshine, often carrying a vessel to take some of it home with me. There was a brook, indeed; but this was different, it was the spring; it was taken home as a beautiful flower might be brought. It is not the physical water, it is the sense or feeling that it conveys. Nor is it the physical sunshine; it is the sense of inexpressible beauty which it brings with it. Of such I still drink, and hope to do so still deeper.

CLEMATIS LANE.

WILD clematis grew so thickly on one side of the
narrow lane that the hedge seemed made of it. Trail-
ing over the low bushes, the leaves hid the hawthorn
and bramble, so that the hedge was covered with
clematis leaf and flower. The innumerable pale flowers
gave out a faint odour, and coloured the sides of the
highway. Rising up the hazel rods and taller hawthorn, the tendrils hung downwards and suspended
the flowers overhead. Across the field, where a hill
rose and was dotted with bushes—these bushes, too,
were concealed by clematis, and though the flowers
were so pale their numbers tinted the slope. A cropped
nut-tree hedge, again, low, but five or six yards thick,
was bound together by the bines of the same creeping
plant, twisting in and out, and holding it together.
No care or art could have led it over the branches in
so graceful a manner ; the lane was festooned for the
triumphal progress of the waggons laden with corn.
Here and there, on the dry bank over which the
clematis projected like an eave, there stood tall cam-
panulas, their blue bells as large as the fingerstall of a
foxglove. The slender purple spires of the climbing
vetch were lifted above the low bushes to which it

clung; there were ferns deeper in the hedge, and yellow bedstraw by the gateways. A few blackberries were ripe, but the clematis seemed to have overcome the brambles, and spoilt their yield. Nuts, reddened at the tip, were visible on the higher hazel boughs; they were ripe, but difficult to get at.

Leaving the lane by a waggon track—a gipsy track through a copse—there were large bunches of pale-red berries hanging from the wayfaring trees, or wild viburnum, and green and red berries of bryony wreathed among the branches. The bryony leaves had turned, some were pale buff already. Among the many berries of autumn those of the wayfaring tree may be known by their flattened shape, as if the sides had been pressed in like a flask. The bushes were not high enough for shadow, and the harvest sun was hot between them. The track led past the foot of a steep headland of the Downs, which could not be left without an ascent. Dry and slippery, the short grass gave no hold to the feet, and it was necessary to step in the holes cut through the turf for the purpose. Pushed forward from the main line of the Downs, the buff headland projected into the Weald, as headlands on the southern side of the range project into the sea. Towards the summit the brow came out somewhat, and even the rude steps in the turf were not much assistance in climbing this almost perpendicular wall of sward. Above the brow the ascent became easy; these brows raised steeper than the general slope are often found on the higher hills. A circular entrenchment encloses the summit, but the rampart has much sunk, and is in places levelled. Here it was pleasant to look back upon the beech woods at the foot of the great Downs, and far over the endless fields of the Weald or plain. Thirty fields could be counted in succession, one after the other, like irregular chess-squares, some corn, some grass, and these only extended to the first undulation, where the woods hid the fields behind them. But beyond these, in reality, succeeded another series of fields to the second undulation, and still a third series to the farthest undulation visible. Yet farther there was a faint line of hills, a dark cloud-like bank in the extreme distance. To the right and to the left were similar views. Reapers were at work in the wheat below, but already much of the corn had been carried, and the hum of a threshing engine came up from the ricks. A woodpecker called loudly in the beech wood; a " wish-wish " in the air overhead was caused by the swift motion of a wood-pigeon passing from "holt" to "hurst," from copse to copse. On the dry short turf of the hill-top even the shadow of a swallow was visible as he flew but a few yards high.

In a little hollow where the rougher grasses grew longer a blue butterfly fluttered and could not get out. He was entangled with his own wings, he could not guide himself between the grass tops; his wings fluttered and carried him back again. The grass was like a net to him, and there he fluttered till the wind lifted him out, and gave him the freedom of the hills. One small green orchis stood in the grass, alone ; the harebells were many. It is curious that, if gathered, in a few hours (if pressed between paper) they become a deeper blue than when growing. Another butterfly went over, large and velvety, flying head to the wind, but unable to make way against it, and so carried sidelong across the current. From the summit of the hill he drifted out into the air five hundred feet above the flowers of the plain. Perhaps it was a peacock; for there was a peacock-butterfly in Clematis Lane. The harebells swung, and the dry tips of the grass bent to the wind which came over the hills from the sea, but from which the sun had dried the sea-moisture, leaving it twice refined—once by the passage above a hundred miles of wave and foam and again by the grasses and the hills, which forced the current to a higher level, where the sunbeams dried it. Twice refined, the air was strong and pure, sweet like the scent of a flower. If the air at the sea beach is good, that of the hills above the sea is at least twice as good, and twice as strengthening. It possesses all the virtue of the sea air without the moisture which ultimately loosens the joints, and seems to penetrate to the very nerves. Those who desire air and quick recovery should go to the hills, where the wind has a scent of the sunbeams.

In the short time since ascending the slope the definition of the view has changed. At first it was clear indeed, and no one would have supposed there was any mist. But now suddenly every hill stands out sharp and definite; the scattered hawthorn bushes are distinct; the hills look higher than before. From about the woods an impalpable bluish mistiness that was there just now has been blown away. The yellow squares of stubble—just cleared—far below are whiter and look drier. I think it is the air that tints every-

G

thing. This fresh stratum now sweeping over has altered the appearance of the country and given me a new scene. The invisible air, as if charged with colour, has spread another tone broadly over the landscape. Omitting no detail, it has worked out afresh every little bough of the scattered hawthorn bushes, and made each twig distinct. It is the air that tints everything.

While I have been thinking, a flock of sheep has stolen quietly into the space enclosed by the entrenchment. With the iron head of his crook placed against his breast, and the handle aslant to the ground, the shepherd leans against it, and looks down upon the reapers. He is a young man, and has a bright, intelligent expression on his features. Alone with his sheep so many hours, he is glad of some one to talk to, and points out to me the various places in view. The copses that cover the slopes of the hills he calls "holts;" there are three or four within a short distance. His crook is not a Pyecombe crook (for the best crooks used to be made at Pyecombe, a little Down hamlet), but he has another, which was made from a Pyecombe pattern. The village craftsman, whose shepherds' crooks were sought for all along the South Downs, is no more, and he has left no one able to carry on his work. He had an apprentice, but the apprentice has taken to another craft, and cannot make crooks. The Pyecombe crook has a curve or semicircle, and then opens straight; the straight part starts at a tangent from the semicircle. How difficult it is to describe so simple a matter as a shepherd's crook! In some way or other this Pyecombe form is found more effective for capturing sheep, but it is

not so easy to make. The crook he held in his hand
opened with an elongated curve. It appeared very
small beside the ordinary crooks; this, he said, was
an advantage, as it would hold a lamb. Another he
showed me had the ordinary hook; this was bought
at Brighton. The curve was too big, and a sheep
could get its leg out; besides which, the iron was soft,
and when a sheep was caught the iron bent and
enlarged, and so let the sheep go. The handles were
of hazel: one handle was straight, smooth, and the best
in appearance—but he said it was weak; the other
handle, which was crooked and rough-looking, was
twice as strong. They used hazel rods for handles—
ash rods were apt to "fly," *i.e.* break.

Wages were now fifteen shillings a week. The "farm
hands"—elsewhere labourers—had fifteen shillings a
week, and paid one shilling and sixpence a week for
their cottages. The new cottages that had been built
were two shillings and sixpence a week. They liked
the old cottages best, not only because they were
cheaper, but because they had larger gardens attached.
It seemed that the men were fairly satisfied with their
earnings; just then, of course, they were receiving
much more for harvest work, such as tying up after
the reaping machine at seven shillings and sixpence
per acre. Clothes were the heaviest item of expendi-
ture, especially where there was a family and the
children were not old enough to earn anything. Except
that he said "wid" for with—"wid" this, instead of
with this—he scarcely mispronounced a word, speaking
as distinctly and expressing himself as clearly as any
one could possibly do. The briskness of manner, quick

apprehension, and directness of answer showed a well-trained mind. The Sussex shepherd on this lonely hill was quite the equal of any man in his rank of life, and superior in politeness to many who move in more civilized places. He left me to fetch some wattles, called flakes in other counties; a stronger sort of hurdles. Most of the reaping is now done by machine, still there were men cutting wheat by hand at the foot of the hill. They call their reaphooks swaphooks, or swophooks, and are of opinion that although the machine answers well and clears the ground quickly when the corn stands up, if it is beaten down the swaphook is preferable. The swaphook is the same as the fagging-hook of other districts. Every hawthorn bush now bears its red berries, or haws; these are called "hog-hazels." In the west they are called "peggles." "Sweel" is an odd Sussex word, meaning to singe linen. People who live towards the hills (which are near the coast) say that places farther inland are more "uperds"—up the country—up towards Tunbridge, for instance.

The grasshoppers sang merrily round me as I sat on the sward; the warm sun and cloudless sky and the dry turf pleased them. Though cloudless, the wind rendered the warmth pleasant, so that the sunbeams, from which there was no shade, were not oppressive. The grasshoppers sang, the wind swept through the grass and swung the harebells, the "drowsy hum" of the threshing engine rose up from the plain; the low slumberous melody of harvest time floated in the air. An hour had gone by imperceptibly before I descended the slope to Clematis Lane. Out in the stubble where the wheat had just been cut, down amongst the dry short stalks of straw, were the light-blue petals of the grey field veronica. Almost the very first of field flowers in the earliest days of spring, when the rain drives over the furrow, and hail may hap at any time, here it was blooming again in the midst of the harvest. Two scenes could scarcely be more dissimilar than the wet and stormy hours of the early year, and the dry, hot time of harvest; the pale blue veronica, with one white petal, flourished in both, true and faithful. The gates beside the lane were not gates at all, but double draw-bars framed together, so that the gate did not open on a hinge, but had to be drawn out of the mortices. Looking over one of these grey and lichened draw-bars in a hazel hedge there were the shocks of wheat standing within the field, and on them a flock of rooks helping themselves freely.

Lower in the valley, where there was water, the tall willow-herbs stood up high as the hedges. On the banks of a pool water-plantains had sent up stalks a yard high, branched, and each branch bearing its three-petalled flower. In a copse near the stems of cow-parsnip stood quite seven feet, drawn up by the willow bushes—these great plants are some of the largest that grow in the country. Goatsbeard grew by the wayside; it is like the dandelion, but has dark spots in the centre of the disc, and the flower shuts at noon. The wild carrots were forming their "birds' nests"— so soon as the flowering is over the umbel closes into the shape of a cup or bird's nest. The flower of the wild carrot is white; it is made up of numerous small separate florets on an umbel, and in the centre of these tiny florets is a deep crimson one. Getting down towards the sea and the houses now I found a shrub of henbane by the dusty road, dusty itself, grey-green, and draggled; I call it a shrub, though a plant because of its shrub-like look. The flowers were over —they are a peculiar colour, dark and green veined and red, there is no exact term for it, but you may know the plant by the leaves, which, if crushed, smell like those of the black currant. This is one of the old English medicinal plants still in use. The figs were ripening fast in an orchard; the fig trees are frequently grown between apple trees, which shelter them, and some of the fruit was enclosed in muslin bags to protect it. The fig orchards along the coast suggest thoughts of Italy and the ancient Roman galleys which crossed the sea to the Sussex ports. There is a curious statement in a classic author, to the effect that a letter written by Julius Cæsar, when in Britain, on the Kalends of September, reached Rome on the fourth day before the Kalends of October, showing how long a letter was being carried from the South Coast to the centre of Italy, nineteen centuries ago.

NATURE NEAR BRIGHTON.

"As wild as a hawk" is a proverbial comparison, but
kestrels venture into the outskirts of Brighton, and
even right over the town. Not long since one was
observed hovering above a field which divides part of
Brighton from Hove. The bird had hardly settled
himself, and obtained his balance, when three or four
rooks who were passing deliberately changed their
course to attack him. Moving with greater swiftness,
the kestrel escaped their angry but clumsy assaults;
still they drove him from the spot, and followed him
eastwards over the town till out of sight—now wheel-
ing round, and now doing their utmost to rise higher
and get the advantage of him. Kestrels appear rather
numerous in this vicinity. Those who have driven
round Brighton and Hove must have noticed the large
stables which have been erected for the convenience of
gentlemen residing in streets where stabling at the
rear of the house is impracticable. Early in the year
a kestrel began to haunt one of these large establishments, notwithstanding that it was much frequented,
carriages driving in and out constantly, hunters taken
to and fro, and in despite of the neighbourhood being
built over with villas. There was a piece of waste

ground by the building where, on a little tree, the
hawk perched day after day.   Then, beating round, he
hovered over the gardens of the district, often above
the public roads and over a large tennis lawn.   His
farthest sweep seemed to be to the Sussex County
Cricket field and then back again.   Day after day he
went his rounds for weeks together, through the
stormy times of the early months, passing several
times a day, almost as regularly as the postman.   He
showed no fear, hovering close to the people in the
roads or working in their gardens.   All his motions
could be observed with facility—the mode of hovering,
which he accomplished easily, whether there was a
gale or a perfect calm ; indeed, his ways could be
noted as well as if it had been by the side of the wildest
copse.   One morning he perched on a chimney; the
house was not occupied, but the next to it was, and
there were builders' workmen engaged on the opposite
side of the road ; so that the wild hawk, if unmolested,
would soon become comparatively tame.   When the
season became less rigorous, and the breeding time
approached, the kestrel was seen no more ; having
flown for the copses between the Downs or in the
Weald.

The power of hovering is not so wonderful as that
of soaring, which the hawks possess, but which is also
exhibited by seagulls.   On a March morning two gulls
came up from the sea, and as they neared the Downs
began to soar.   It was necessary to fix the gaze on
one, as the eyes cannot follow two soaring birds at
once.   This gull, having spread his wings wide, swept
up the dean, or valley, with great speed, and, turning

a large circle, rose level with the hill. Round again he came, rising spirally—a spiral with a diameter varying from a furlong to a quarter of a mile, sometimes wider—and was now high overhead. Turn succeeded turn, up, up, and this without a single movement of the wings, which were held extended and rigid. The edge of the wing on the outer side was inclined to the horizon—one wing elevated, the other depressed—as the bird leaned inwards like a train going round a curve. The plane of the wings glided up the air as, with no apparent diminution of speed from friction, the bird swiftly ascended. Fourteen times the bird swept round, never so much as moving his wings, till now the gaze could no longer distinguish his manner of progress. The white body was still perceptible, but the wings were indistinct. Up to that height the gull had not assisted his ascent by flapping, or striking the air in any way. The original impulse, and some hitherto unexplained elasticity or property of air, had sufficed to raise him, in apparent defiance of the retardation of friction, and of the drag of gravitation. This power of soaring is the most wonderful of the various problems of flight being accomplished without effort; and yet, according to our preconceived ideas, there must be force somewhere to cause motion. There was a moderate air moving at the time, but it must be remembered that if a wind assists one way it retards the other.* Hawks can certainly soar in the calmest weather.

One day I saw a weasel cross a road in Hove, close to a terrace of houses.

* See the paper on "Birds Climbing the Air."

It is curious that a seagull can generally be observed opposite the Aquarium; when there is no seagull elsewhere along the whole Brighton front there is often one there. Young gulls occasionally alight on the roof, or are blown there. Once now and then a porpoise may be seen sunning himself off a groyne; barely dipping himself, and rolling about at the surface, the water shines like oil as it slips off his back.

The Brighton rooks are house birds, like sparrows, and perch on the roofs or chimneys—there are generally some on the roof of the Église Reformée Française, a church situated in a much-frequented part. It is amusing to see a black rook perched on a red tile chimney, with the smoke coming up around him, and darkening with soot his dingy plumage. They take every scrap thrown out, like sparrows, and peck bones if they find them. The builders in Brighton appear to have somewhat overshot the mark, to judge from the number of empty houses, and, indeed, it is currently reported that it will be five years before the building speculation recovers itself. Upon these empty houses, the hoardings, and scaffold-poles, the rooks perch exactly as if they were trees in a hedgerow, waiting with comic gravity to pounce on anything in the gardens or on the lawns. They are quite aware when it is Sunday—on week-days they keep at a fair distance from workmen; on Sundays they drop down in places where at other times they do not dare to venture, so that a glove might be thrown out of window among them. In winter and spring there are rooks everywhere; as summer advances, most leave the town for the fields.

A marked sign of spring in Brighton is the return of the wheatears ; they suddenly appear in the waste places by the houses in the first few days of April. Wheatears often run a considerable distance on the sward very swiftly, usually stopping on some raised spot of the turf. Meadow-pipits are another spring bird here ; any one going up the Dyke Road in early spring will observe a little brown bird singing in the air much like a lark, but more feebly. He only rises to a certain height, and then descends in a slanting direction, singing, to the ground. The meadow-pipit is, apparently, uncertain where he shall come down, wandering and irregular on his course. Many of them finish their song in the gardens of the Convent of the Sacred Heart, which seem to be a refuge to birds. At least, the thrushes sing there sweetly—yellow-hammers, too—on the high wall. There is another resort of birds, opposite the Convent, on the Stanford Estate, on which persons are warned not to shoot or net small birds. A little shrubbery there in April and May is full of thrushes, blackbirds, and various finches, all happily singing, and busy at their nests. Here the birds sing both sides of the highway, despite the reproach that Brighton is bare of trees ; they pass from the shrubbery to and from the Convent gardens.

It is to be wished that these notices not to shoot or net small birds were more frequently seen. Brighton is still a bird-catching centre, and before the new close season commences acres of ground are covered with the nets of the bird-catchers. Pity they could not be confined a little while in the same manner as they confine their miserable feathery victims (in cages just to fit the bird, say six inches square) in cells where movement or rest would be alike impossible. Yet goldfinches are still to be seen close to the town; they are fond of the seeds which they find wherever there is a waste place, and on the slopes of unfinished roads. Each unoccupied house, and many occupied, has its brood of starlings; a starling the other day was taking insects from the surface of a sheep pond on the hill, flying out to the middle of the pond and snatching the insects from the water. During the long weeks of rain and stormy weather in the spring of 1883, the Downs looked dreary indeed; open, unsheltered, the grass so short as scarcely to be called grass, wet and slippery. But a few glimpses of sunshine soon brought a change. Where the furze bushes had been cut down, the stems of furze began to shoot, looking at a little distance like moss on the ground. Among these there were broad violet patches —scentless violets, nothing to gather, but pleasant to see—colouring the earth. Presently the gorse flowered, miles of it, and the willow wrens sang plaintively among it. The brightest bird on the Downs was then the stonechat. Perched on a dead thistle, his blackest of black heads, the white streak by his neck, and the brilliance of his colouring contrasted with the yellow gorse around. In the hedges on the northern slopes of the Downs, towards the Weald, or plain, the wayfaring tree grows in large shrubs, blooming among the thorns.

The banks by Brighton in early spring are purple with the flowers of ground ivy, which flowers with exceptional freedom. One bank, or waste spot, that was observed was first of all perfectly purple with ground ivy; by degrees these flowers faded, and the spot became a beautiful blue with veronica, or bird's-eye; then, again, these disappeared, and up came the larger daisies on stalks a foot high, whose discs touched each other from end to end of the bank. Here was a succession of flowers as if designed, one taking the other's place. Meantime the trifolium appeared like blood spilt among the grass.

The thin, chalky soil of Sussex is singularly favourable to poppies and charlock—the one scarlet, the other a sharp yellow; they cover acres. Wild pansies flowered on the hillside fallows, high up among the wind, where the notes of the cuckoo came faint from the wood in the Weald beneath. The wind threw back the ringing notes, but every now and then, as the breeze ebbed, they came, having travelled a full mile against the current of air. There is no bird with so powerful a voice as the cuckoo; his cry can be heard almost as far as a clarion. The wild pansies were very thick—little yellow petals streaked with black lines. In a western county the cottagers call them "Loving Idols," which may perhaps be a distortion of the name they bore in Shakespeare's time—"Love in Idleness." It appears as if the rabbits on the chalk are of a rather greyish hue, perceptibly less sandy in colour than those living in meadows on low ground. Though Brighton is bare of trees, there is a large wood at a short distance. It is principally of beech. In this particular wood there is a singular absence of the jays which elsewhere make so much noise. Early in the spring there did not seem a jay in it. They make their appearance in the nesting season and are then trapped. A thrush's nest with eggs in it having been found, a little platform of sticks is built before the nest and a trap placed on it. The jay is so fond of eggs he cannot resist these; he alights on the platform in front of the nest, and is so captured. The bait of an egg will generally succeed in drawing a jay to his destruction. A good deal of poaching goes on about Brighton at Christmas time, when the coverts are full of game.

The Downs as they trend along the coast now recede and now approach, now sink in deans, then rise abruptly, topped with copses which, like Lancing Clump, are visible many miles both at sea and on land. Between them and the beach there lies a rich alluvial belt, narrow and flat, much of which appears to have been reclaimed by drainage from the condition of marsh, and which, in fact, presents a close similitude to the fens. Here, in the dykes, the aquatic grasses reach a great height, and the flowering rush grows. It is said that this land is sought after among agriculturists, and that those who occupy it have escaped better than the majority from the pressure of bad seasons. Somewhat away from the present coast-line, where the hills begin—perhaps the sea came as far inland once—may be found ancient places, still ports, with histories running back into the mythic period. Passing through such a place on a sunny day in the earlier part of the year, the extreme quiet and air of silence were singularly opposite to the restlessness of the great watering-place near. It was but a few steps

out into the wooded country. Yellow wallflowers
grew along the high wall, and flowered against the
sky; swallows flew to and fro the warm space
sheltered from the wind, beneath them. In the lane
a blackbird was so occupied among the arums at the
roots of the trees that he did not stir till actually
obliged. Blackbirds and thrushes are fond of searching about where the arums grow thickest. In the
park a clump of tall aspens gleamed like silk in the
sunshine. The calls of moorhens came up from a lake
in a deep valley near, beeches grow down the steep
slope to the edge of the water, and the wind which
rippled it drew in a strong draught up the hill. From
that height the glance saw to the bottom of the clear
water, to which the waves and the wind gave a trans-
lucent green. The valley winds northward, curving
like a brook, and in the trough a narrow green band
of dark grass follows the windings, a pathlike ribbon
as deeply coloured as a fairy ring, and showing between the slopes of pale turf. On this side are copses
of beech, and on that of fir; the fir copses are encircled
by a loose hedge of box, fading and yellowish, while
the larch tops were filled with sweet and tender green.
Like the masts and yards of a ship, which are
gradually hidden as the sails are set, so these green
sails unfurling concealed the tall masts and taper
branches of the fir. Afar the great hills were bare,
wind-swept and dry. The glass-green river wound
along the plain, and the sea bloomed blue under the
sun, blue by the distant shore, darkening like a level
cloud where a dim ship marked the horizon. A blue
sky requires greensward and green woods—the sward

is pale and the woods are slow; the cuckoo calls for his leaves.

Farther along the edge of the valley the beeches thicken, and the turf is covered by the shrunken leaves of last year. Empty hulls of beechmast crunch under foot, the brown beech leaves have drifted a foot deep against the trunk of a felled tree. Beech leaves lie at rest in the cover of furze, sheltered from the wind; suddenly a little cloud of earth rises like dust as a startled cock pheasant scrambles on his wings with a scream. A hen follows, and rises steadily in a long-drawn slanting line till near the tops of the beeches, then rockets sharp up over the highest branches, and descends in a wide sweeping curve along the valley. In the glade among the beeches the furze has grown straight up ten feet high, like sapling trees, and flowers at the top, golden bloom on a dry pole. There are more pheasants in the furze, so that, not to disturb them, it is best to walk round and not enter it. Every now and then there is a curious, half-finished note among the trees—yuc, yuc. This great hawthorn has a twisted stem; the wood winds round itself in a spiral. The bole of a beech in the sunshine is spotted like a trout by the separate shadows of its first young leaves. Tall bushes—almost trees—of blackthorn are in full white flower; the dark, leafless boughs make it appear the whiter. Among the black-thorn several tits are busy, searching about on the twigs, and pecking into the petals; calling loudly as they do so. A willow-wren is peering into the bloom, too, but silent for the moment. The blackthorn is much lichened, the lichen which is built into the domed nest of the long-tailed titmouse. Yuc—yuc, again. Stalks of spurge, thickening towards the top, and then surrounded with leaves, and above these dull yellow-green flowers, grow in shrub-like bunches in more open ground. Among the shrunken leaves on the turf here and there are the white flowers of the barren strawberry. A green woodpecker starts from a tree, and can be watched between the trunks as he flies; his bright colour marks him. Presently, on rounding some furze, he rises again, this time from the ground, and goes over the open glade; flying, the green woodpecker appears a larger bird than would be supposed if seen when still. He has been among the beeches all the time, and it was his "Yuc, yuc" which we heard. Where the woodpecker is heard and seen, there the woods are woods and wild—a sense of wildness accompanies his presence.

Across the valley the straight shadows of firs rise up the slope, all drawn in the same direction, parallel on the sward. Far in a hollow of the rounded hill a herd of deer are resting; the plain lies beneath them, and beyond it the sea. Though they rest in a hollow the green hill is open above and below them; they do not dread the rifle, but if they did they would be safe there. Returning again through the woods, there are some bucks lying on a pleasant sunny slope. Almost too idle to rise, they arch their backs, and stretch their legs, as much as to say, Why trouble us? The wind rushes through the trees, and draws from them strange sounds, now a groan, now almost a shriek, as the boughs grind against each other and wear the bark away. From a maple a twisted ivy basket hangs filled

H

with twigs, leaves, and tree dust, big as three rooks' nests.   Only recently a fine white-tailed eagle was soaring over the woods; he may have followed the line of the sea down from the Hebrides.   Up from the sea comes the wind, drawing swifter between the beech trunks, resting a little in the sunny glades, on again into the woods.   The glass-green river yonder coloured by the wind runs on seaward, there are thin masts of ships visible at its mouth miles away, the wind whistles in their shrouds; beyond the blue by the shore, far, far distant on the level cloud, the dim ship has sailed along the horizon.   It dries the pale grass, and rustles the restless shrunken leaves on the ground; it dries the grey lichen on the beech trunks; it swings the fledglings in the rooks' nests, and carries the ring-dove on a speedier wing.   Blackbirds whistle all around, the woods are full of them; willow-wrens plaintively sing in the trees; other birds call—the dry wind mingles their notes.   It is a hungry wind—it makes a wanderer as hungry as Robin Hood; it drives him back to the houses, and there by a door-step lies a heap of bucks'-horns thrown down like an armful of wood.

SEA, SKY, AND DOWN.

IN the cloudless January sky the sun at noonday
appears high above the southern horizon, and there is
a broad band of sky between it and the line of the sea.
This sense of the sun's elevation is caused by the level
plain of water, which affords no contrast. Inland the
hills rise up, and even at midday the sun in winter does
not seem much above their ridges. But here by the
shore the sun hangs high, and does not look as if he
descended so low in his winter curve. There is little
wind, and the wavelets swing gently rather than roll,
illumined both in their hollows and on their crests
with a film of silver. Three or four miles away a
vessel at anchor occasionally sways, and at each movement flashes a bright gleam from her wet side like a
mirror. White gulls hawk to and fro by the strand,
darting on floating fragments and rising again; their
plumage is snowy white in the sunshine. Brown nets
lie on the pebbles; brown nets are stretched from the
mastheads of the smacks to the sea-wall; brown and
deeply wrinkled sails are hoisted to dry in the sun
and air. The broad red streaks on the smacks' sides
stand out distinctly among the general pitchy hues
of gunwales and great coils of rope. Men in dull

yellow tan frocks are busy round about among them,
some mending nets, some stooping over a boat turned
bottom upwards, upon which a patch is being placed.
It needs at least three or four men to manage this
patch properly. These tan frocks vary from a dull
yellow to a copperish red colour. A golden vane high
overhead points to the westward, and the dolphin, with
open mouth, faces the light breeze.

Under the groynes there is shadow as in summer;
once and again the sea runs up and breaks on the beach,
and the foam, white as the whitest milk, hisses as it
subsides among the pebbles; it effervesces and bubbles
at the brim of the cup of the sea. Farther along the
chalk cliffs stand up clear and sharp, the green sea
beneath, and the blue sky above them. There is a light
and colour everywhere, the least fragment of colour is
brought out, even the worn red tiles washed smooth by
the tides and rolled over and over among the pebbles,
the sea gleams, and there is everything of summer but
the heat. Reflected in the plate-glass windows of the
street the sea occupies the shop front, covering over
the golden bracelets and jewellery with a moving
picture of the silvery waves. The day is lengthened
by the light, and dark winter driven away, till, the
sun's curve approaching the horizon, misty vapours
begin to thicken in the atmosphere where they had
not been suspected. The tide is out, and for miles the
foam runs in on the level sands, forming a long succession of graceful curves marked with a white edge.

As the sun sinks, the wet sands are washed with a
brownish yellow, the colour of ripe wheat if it could
be supposed liquid. The sunset, which has begun

with pale hues, flushes over a rich violet, soon again
overlaid with orange, and succeeded in its turn by a
deep red glow—a glow which looks the deeper the
more it is gazed at, like a petal of peony. There are
no fair faces in the street now, they are all brunettes,
fair complexions and dark skins are alike tinted by the
sunset; they are all swarthy. On the sea a dull redness reaches away and is lost in the vapour on the
horizon; eastwards great vapours, tinged rosy, stand up
high in the sky, and seem to drift inland, carrying the
sunset with them; presently the atmosphere round the
houses is filled with a threatening light, like a great
fire reflected over the housetops. It fades, and there
is nothing left but a dark cloud at the western horizon,
tinted blood-red along its upper edge. Next morning
the sun rises, a ball of orange amid streaks of scarlet.

But sometimes the sunset takes other order than
this, and after the orange there appears a rayed
scarlet crown, such as one sees on old coins—rays of
scarlet shoot upward from a common centre above
where the sun went down. Sometimes, instead of
these brilliant hues, there is the most delicate shading
of pearly greys and nameless silver tints, such tints as
might be imagined were the clouds like feathers, the
art of which is to let the under hue shine through the
upper layer of the plumage. Though not so gaudy or
at first so striking, these pearl-greys, and silvers, and
delicate interweaving of tints are really as wonderful,
being graduated and laid on with a touch no camel's
hair can approach. Sometimes, again, the sunset shows
a burnished sky, like the surface of old copper burnt
or oxidized—the copper tinted with rose, or with rose

and violet. During the prevalence of the scarlet and orange hues, the moon, then young, shining at the edge of the sunset, appeared faintly green; and people remarked how curious a green moon looked on a blue sky, for it was just where the sunset vapour melted into the upper sky. At the same moment the gas-lamps burned green—rows and rows of pale green lights. As the sunset faded both the moon and gas-lamps took their proper hue; hence it appeared as if the change of colour were due to contrast. The gas-lamps had looked greenish several evenings before the new moon shone, and in their case there can be no doubt the tint was contrast merely. One night, some hours after sunset, and long after the last trace of it had disappeared, the moon was sailing through light white clouds, which only partly concealed her, and was sur-rounded by the ordinary prismatic halo. But outside this halo there was a green circle, a broad green band, very distinct—a pale emerald green. Beautiful and interesting as these sunsets have been, I cannot sub-scribe to the opinion that they surpass all that have been observed; for I distinctly remember sunsets equally brilliant, and some even more so, which occurred not so very long ago. To those who are in the habit of observing out-of-door phenomena a beauti-ful sunset is by no means uncommon.

Sometimes the sea disappears under the haze of the winter's day: it is fine, but hazy, and from the hills, looking southwards, the sea seems gone, till, the sun breaking out, two or three horizontal streaks reflected suddenly reveal its surface. Another time the reflec-tion of the sun's rays takes the form of a gigantic and exaggerated hour-glass; by the shore the reflection widens out, narrows as it recedes to a mere path, and again at the horizon widens and fills a mile or more. Then at the horizon the lighted sea seems raised above the general level. Rain is approaching, and then by the beach the sea becomes yellowish, beyond that green, and a hard blue at the horizon; there is one lovely streak of green on the right; in front a broad spot of sunlight where the clouds have parted. The wind sings, and a schooner is working rapidly out to windward for more room. During changeable weather the sky between the clouds occasionally takes a pale yellow hue, like that of the tinted paper used for drawing. This colour is opaque, and evidently depends upon the presence of thin vapour. It is seen when the wind is in the act of changing its direction, and the clouds, arrested in their march, are thrown out of rank. That which was the side becomes the rear of the cloud, and is banked up by the sudden pressure. Clouds coming in from the sea are met with a land wind, and so diverted. The effect of mist on the sea in the dark winter days is to increase distances, so that a ship at four or five miles appears hull down, and her shadowy sails move in vapour almost as thick as the canvas. At evening there is no visible sunset, but presently the whole sky, dull and gloomy, is suffused with a redness, not more in one part than another, but over the entire heavens. So in the clouded mornings, a deep red hue fills the whole dome.

But if the sun rises clear, the rays light up the yellow sand of the quarries inland, the dark brown ploughed fields, and the black copses where many a bud is sleeping and waiting for the spring. A haze lies about the Downs and softens their smooth outline as in summer, if you can but face the bleak wind which never rests up there. The outline starts on the left hand fairly distinguished against the sky. As it sweeps round, it sinks, and is lost in the bluish haze; gradually it rises again, and is visible on the right, where the woods stand leafless on the ridge. Or the vapour settles down thicker, and the vast expanse becomes gloomy in broad day. The formless hills loom round about, the roads and marks of civilization seem blotted out, it may be some absolute desert for aught that appears. An immense hollow filled with mist lies underneath. Presently the wind drifts the earth-cloud along, and there by a dark copse are three or four horsemen eagerly seeking a way through the plantation. They are two miles distant, but as plainly visible as if you could touch them. By-and-by one finds a path, and in single file the troop rides into the wood. On the other side there is a long stretch of open ploughed field, and about the middle of it little white dots close together, sweeping along as if the wind drove them. Horsemen are galloping on the turf at the edge of the arable, which is doubtless heavy going. The troop that has worked through the wood labours hard to overtake; the vapour follows again, and horsemen and hounds are lost in the abyss.

On a ridge closer at hand, and above the mist, stand two conical wheat ricks sharply defined—all that a draughtsman could seize on. Still, even in winter there is about the hills the charm of outline, and the uncertain haze produces some of the effects of summer, but it is impossible to stay and admire, the penetrating wind will permit of nothing except hard exercise. Looking back now and then, the distant hollows are sometimes visible and sometimes filled; great curtains of mist sweep along illumined by the sunlight above them; the woods are now brown, now dark, and now faintly blue, as the light changes. Over the range and down in the valley where the hursts or woods are situated, surrounded by meads and cornfields, there are other notes of colour to be found. In the leafless branches of the oak sometimes the sunshine plays on the bark of the smaller boughs, and causes a sense of light and colour among them. The slender boughs of the birch, too, reflect the sunshine as if polished. Beech leaves still adhere to the lower branches, spots of bright brown among the grey and ash tint of the under-wood. If a woodpecker passes, his green plumage gleams the more from the absence of the abundant foliage which partly conceals even him in summer. The light-coloured wood-pigeons show distinctly against the dark firs; the golden crest of the tiny wren is to be seen in the furze or bramble.

All broader effects of colour must in winter be looked for in the atmosphere, as the light changes, as the mist passes, as the north wind brings down a blackness, or the gust dries up the furrow; as the colour of the air alters, for it is certain that the air is often full of colour. To the atmosphere we must look for all broader effects. Specks of detail may be sometimes discerned, one or two in a walk, as the white breasts of the lapwings on the dark ploughed ridges; yellow oat-straw by the farm, still retaining the golden tint of summer; if fortunate, a blue kingfisher by the brook, and always dew flashing emerald and ruby.

JANUARY IN THE SUSSEX WOODS.

THE lost leaves measure our years; they are gone as the days are gone, and the bare branches silently speak of a new year, slowly advancing to its buds, its foliage, and fruit. Deciduous trees associate with human life as this yew never can. Clothed in its yellowish-green needles, its tarnished green, it knows no hope or sorrow; it is indifferent to winter, and does not look forward to summer. With their annual loss of leaves, and renewal, oak and elm and ash and beech seem to stand by us and to share our thoughts. There is no wind at the edge of the wood, and the few flakes of snow that fall from the overcast sky flutter as they drop, now one side higher and then the other, as the leaves did in the still hours of autumn. The delicacy of the outer boughs of the great trees visible against the dark background of cloud is as beautiful in its own way as the massed foliage of summer. Each slender bough is drawn out to a line; line follows line as shade grows under the pencil, but each of these lines is separate. Great bòles of beech, heavy timber at the foot, thus end at their summits in the lightest and most elegant pencilling. Where the birches are tall, sometimes the number and closeness of these bare sprays causes a thickening almost as if there were leaves there. The leaves, in fact, when they come, conceal the finish of the trees; they give colour, but they hide the beautiful structure under them. Each tree at a distance is recognizable by its particular lines; the ash, for instance, grows with its own marked curve.

Some flakes of snow have remained on this bough of spruce, pure white on dull green. Sparingly dispersed, the snow can be seen falling far ahead between the trunks; indeed, the white dots appear to increase the distance the eye can penetrate; it sees farther because there is something to catch the glance. Nothing seems left for food in the woods for bird or animal. Some ivy berries and black privet berries remain, a few haws may be found; for the rest, it is gone; the squirrels have had the nuts, the acorns were taken by the jays, rooks, and pheasants. Bushels of acorns, too, were collected by hand as food for the fallow deer in the park. A great fieldfare rises, like a lesser pigeon; fieldfares often haunt the verge of woods, while the redwing thrushes go out into the meadows. It can scarcely be doubted that both these birds come over to escape the keener cold of the winters in Norway, or that the same cause drives the blackbirds hither. In spring we listen to Norwegian songs—the blackbird and the thrush that please us so much, if not themselves of Scandinavian birth, have had a Scandinavian origin. Any one walking about woods like these in January can understand how, where there are large flocks of birds, they must find the pressure of numbers through the insufficiency of food. They go then to

seek a warmer climate and more to eat; more particularly probably for sustenance.

The original and simple theory that the majority of
birds migrate for food or warmth is not overthrown
by modern observations. That appears to be the
primary impulse, though others may be traced or
reasonably imagined. To suppose, as has been put
forward, that birds are endowed with a migratory
instinct for the express purpose of keeping down
their numbers, in order, that is, that they may perish
in crossing the sea, is really too absurd for serious
consideration. If that were the end in view, it would
be most easily obtained by keeping them at home,
where snow would speedily starve them. On the
contrary, it will appear to any one who walks about
woods and fields that migration is essential to the
preservation of these creatures. By migration, in
fact, the species is kept in existence, and room is
found for life. Apart from the necessity of food,
movement and change is one of the most powerful
agencies in renewing health. This we see in our
own experience; the condition of the air is especially
important, and it is well within reasonable supposition that some birds and animals may wish to avoid
certain states of atmosphere. There is, too, the
question of moulting and change of plumage, and the
possibility that this physiological event may influence
the removal to a different climate. Birds migrate
principally for food and warmth; secondly, on account
of the pressure of numbers (for in good seasons they
increase very fast); thirdly, for the sake of health;
fourthly, for sexual reasons; fifthly, from the operation

of a kind of prehistoric memory; sixthly, from choice. One or other of these causes will explain almost every case of migration.

Birds are lively and intellectual, imaginative and affectionate creatures, and all their movements are not dictated by mere necessity. They love the hedge and bush where they were born, they return to the same tree, or the same spot under the eave. On the other hand, they like to roam about the fields and woods, and some of them travel long distances during the day. When the pleasurable cares of the nest are concluded, it is possible that they may in some cases cross the sea solely for the solace of change. Variety of food is itself a great pleasure. By prehistoric memory is meant the unconscious influence of ancient habit impressed upon the race in times when the conformation of land and sea and the conditions of life were different. No space is left for a mysterious agency; migration is purely natural, and acts for the general preservation. Try to put yourself in a bird's place, and you will see that migration is very natural indeed. If at some future period of the world's history men should acquire the art of flying, there can be no doubt that migration would become the custom, and whole nations would change their localities. Man has, indeed, been always a migratory animal. History is little beyond the record of migrations, how one race moved on and overcame the race in front of it. In ancient days lots were cast as to who should migrate, and those chosen by this conscription left their homes that the rest remaining might have room and food. Checking the attempted migration of the Helvetii was

the beginning of Cæsar's exploits. What men do only
at intervals birds do frequently, having greater freedom of movement.

Who can doubt that the wild fowl come south
because the north is frozen over ? The Laplander and
the reindeer migrate together; the Tartars migrate
all the year through, crossing the steppes in winding
and devious but fixed paths, paths settled for each
family, and kept without a map, though invisible to
strangers. It is only necessary to watch the common
sparrow. In spring his merry chirp and his few notes
of song are heard on the roof or in the garden ; here
he spends his time till the broods are reared and the
corn is ripe. Immediately he migrates into the fields.
By degrees he is joined by those left behind to rear
second broods, and at last the stubble is crowded with
sparrows, such flocks no one would believe possible
unless they had seen them. He has migrated for food,
for his food changes with the season, being mainly
insects in spring, and grain and seeds in autumn.
Something may, I venture to think, in some cases of
migration, be fairly attributed to the influence of a
desire for change, a desire springing from physiological
promptings for the preservation of health.   I am
personally subject twice a year to the migratory impulse.   I feel it in spring and autumn, say about
March, when the leaves begin to appear, and again
as the corn is carried, and most strongly as the
fields are left in stubble. I have felt it every year
since boyhood, often so powerfully as to be quite
unable to resist it. Go I must, and go I do, somewhere; if I do not I am soon unwell. The general

idea of direction is southerly, both spring and autumn; no doubt the reason is because this is a northern country.

Some little green stays on the mounds where the rabbits creep and nibble the grasses. Cinquefoil remains green though faded, and wild parsley the freshest looking of all; plantain leaves are found under shelter of brambles, and the dumb nettles, though the old stalks are dead, have living leaves at the ground. Grey-veined ivy trails along, here and there is a frond of hart's-tongue fern, though withered at the tip, and greenish grey lichen grows on the exposed stumps of trees. These together give a green tint to the mound, which is not so utterly devoid of colour as the season of the year might indicate. Where they fail, brown brake fern fills the spaces between the brambles; and in a moist spot the bunches of rushes are composed half of dry stalks, and half of green. Stems of willow-herb, four feet high, still stand, and tiny long-tailed tits perch sideways on them. Above, on the bank, another species of willow-herb has died down to a short stalk, from which springs a living branch, and at its end is one pink flower. A dandelion is opening on the same sheltered bank; farther on the gorse is sprinkled with golden spots of bloom. A flock of greenfinches starts from the bushes, and their colour shows against the ruddy wands of the osier-bed over which they fly. The path winds round the edge of the wood, where a waggon track goes up the hill; it is deeply grooved at the foot of the hill. These tracks wear deeply into the chalk just where the ascent begins. The chalk adheres to the shoes like mortar,

and for some time after one has left it each footstep
leaves a white mark on the turf. On the ridge the
low trees and bushes have an outline like the flame
of a candle in a draught—the wind has blown them
till they have grown fixed in that shape. In an oak
across the ploughed field a flock of wood-pigeons
have settled; on the furrows there are chaffinches, and
larks rise and float a few yards farther away. The
snow has ceased, and though there is no wind on the
surface, the clouds high above have opened somewhat,
not sufficient for the sun to shine, but to prolong the
already closing afternoon a few minutes. If the sun
shines to-morrow morning the lark will soar and sing,
though it is January, and the quick note of the chaffinch will be heard as he perches on the little branches
projecting from the trunks of trees below the great
boughs. Thrushes sing every mild day in December
and January, entirely irrespective of the season, also
before rain.

A curious instance of a starling having a young
brood at this time of the year, recently recorded, seems
to suggest that birds are not really deceived by the
passing mildness of a few days, but are obliged to
prepare nests, finding themselves in a condition to
require them. The cause, in short, is physiological,
and not the folly of the bird. This starling had had
two previous broods, one in October, and now again in
December-January. The starling was not, therefore, deceived by the chance of mild weather; her own bodily
condition led her to the nest, and had she been a robin
or thrush she would have built one instead of resort-
ing to a cranny. It is certain that individuals among

Birds and animals do occasionally breed at later periods than is usual for the generality of their species. Exceptionally prolific individuals among birds continue to breed into the winter. They are not egregiously deceived any more than we are by a mild interval; the nesting is caused by their individual temperament.

The daylight has lingered on longer than expected, but now the gloom of the short January evening is settling down fast in the wood. The silent and motionless trees rise out of a mysterious shadow, which fills up the spaces between their trunks. Only above, where their delicate outer branches are shown against the dark sky, is there any separation between them. Somewhere in the deep shadow of the underwood a blackbird calls "ching, ching" before he finally settles himself to roost. In the yew the lesser birds are already quiet, sheltered by the evergreen spray; they have also sought the ivy-grown trunks. "Twit, twit," sounds high overhead as one or two belated little creatures, scarcely visible, pass quickly for the cover of the furze on the hill. The short January evening is of but a few minutes' duration; just now it was only dusky, and already the interior of the wood is impenetrable to the glance. There rises a loud though distant clamour of rooks and daws, who have restlessly moved in their roost-trees. Darkness is almost on them, yet they cannot quite settle. The cawing and dawing rises to a pitch, and then declines; the wood is silent, and it is suddenly night.

BY THE EXE.

THE whortleberry bushes are almost as thick as the heather in places on the steep, rocky hills that overlook the Exe. Feeding on these berries when half ripe is said to make the heath poults thin (they are acid), so that a good crop of whortleberries is not advantageous to the black game. Deep in the hollow the Exe winds and bends, finding a crooked way among the ruddy rocks. Sometimes an almost inaccessible precipice rises on one shore, covered with firs and ferns, which no one can gather; while on the other is a narrow but verdant strip of mead. Coming down in flood from the moors the Exe will not wait to run round its curves, but rushes across the intervening corner, and leaves behind, as it subsides, a mass of stones, flat as slates or scales, destroying the grass. But the fly-fisherman seeks the spot because the water is swift at the angle of the stream and broken by a ledge of rock. He can throw up stream—the line falls soft as silk on the slow eddy below the rock, and the fly is drawn gently towards him across the current. When a natural fly approaches the surface of running water, and flutters along just above it, it encounters a light air, which flows in the same direction as the stream. Facing this surface breeze, the fly cannot progress straight up the river, but is carried sideways across it. This motion the artificial fly imitates; a trout takes it, and is landed on the stones. He is not half a pound, yet in the sunshine has all the beauty of a larger fish. Spots of cochineal and gold dust, finely mixed together, dot his sides; they are not red nor yellow exactly, as if gold dust were mixed with some bright red. A line is drawn along his glistening greenish side, and across this there are faintly marked lozenges of darker colour, so that in swimming past he would appear barred. There are dark spots on the head between the eyes, the tail at its lower and upper edges is pinkish; his gills are bright scarlet. Proportioned and exquisitely shaped, he looks like a living arrow, formed to shoot through the water. The delicate little creature is finished in every detail, painted to the utmost minutiæ, and carries a wonderful store of force, enabling him to easily surmount the rapids.

Exe and Barle are twin streams, parted only by a ridge of heather-grown moor. The Barle rises near a place called Simons' Bath, about which there is a legend recalling the fate of Captain Webb. There is a pool at Simons' Bath, in which is a small whirlpool. The stream running in does not seem of much strength; but the eddy is sufficient to carry a dog down. By report the eddy is said to be unfathomable. A long time since a man named Simons thought he could swim through the whirlpool, much as Captain Webb thought he could float down the rapids of Niagara; only in this case Simons relied on the insignificant character of the eddy. He made the attempt, was sucked down and drowned, and hence the spot has been since known as Simons' Bath. So runs the tradition in the neighbourhood, varied in details by different narrators, but not so apocryphal, perhaps, as the story of the two giants, or demons, who amused themselves one day throwing stones, to see which could throw furthest. Their stones were huge boulders; the first pitched his pebble across the Bristol Channel into Wales; the second's foot slipped, and his boulder dropped on Exmoor, where it is known as White Stones to this day. The antiquarians refer Simons' Bath to one Sigmund, but the country-side tradition declares it was named from a man who was drowned. Exe and Barle presently mingle their streams by pleasant oak woods.

At the edge of one of these woods the trench, in the early summer, was filled with ferns, so that, instead of thorns and brambles, the wood was fenced with their green fronds. Among these ferns were some buttercups, at least so they looked in passing; but a slight difference of appearance induced me to stop, and on getting across the trench the buttercups were found to be yellow Welsh poppies. The petals are larger than those of the buttercup, and a paler yellow, without the metallic burnish of the ranunculus. In the centre is the seed vessel, somewhat like an urn; indeed, the yellow poppy resembles the scarlet field poppy, though smaller in width of petal and much more local in habitat. So concealed were the stalks by the ferns that the flowers appeared to grow on their fronds. On the mounds grew corn marigolds, so brilliantly yellow that they seemed to shine in the sunlight, and on a wall moth-mullein flowered high above the foxgloves.

It was curious to hear the labouring people say, "There's the guckoo," when the cuckoo cried. They said he called "guckoo;" so cuckoo sounded to their ears. There are numbers of birds of prey in the oak woods which everywhere grow on the slopes of the Exmoor hills. The keeper who wishes to destroy a whole brood of jays (which take the eggs of game) waits till the young birds are fledged. He then catches one, or wounds it, and, hiding himself in the bushes, pinches it till the bird cries "scaac, scaac." At the sound the old birds come, and are shot as they approach. The fledglings could, of course, be easily destroyed; the object is to get at the wary old jays, and prevent their returning next year. Now and then a buzzard is shot, and if it be only wounded the gunner conceals himself and pinches it till it calls, when the bird's partner presently appears, and is also killed. Stoats are plentiful. They have their young in burrows, or in holes and crevices among the stones, which are found in quantities in the woods. As any one passes such a heap of stones the young stoats peep from the crevices and cry " yac, yac," like barking, and so betray their presence. Three or four traps are set in a circle round the spot, baited with pieces of rabbit, in which the old stoats are soon caught. The young stoats in a day or two, not being fed, come out of the stones, and are shot, or knocked on the head. The woods are always on the sheltered slopes of the hills, the moors on the summits are bare of trees; yet it

would seem that trees once grew there, trunks of oak
being occasionally dug up from the peat. Both the
peaty turf and the heather are used for fuel; the
heather is pulled up, the turf cut with a particular
kind of spade, heart-shaped and pointed, not unlike
the traditional spade used by the gravedigger in
" Hamlet," but with a very long curved handle.

Vipers are sometimes encountered among the heather
where it is sandy. A viper will sometimes wind itself
round the stem of a thorn bush, and thus, turning its
head in every direction, defy a dog. Whichever side
the dog approaches, the viper turns its venomous head.
Dogs frequently kill them, and are sometimes bitten,
generally in the face, when the dog's head swells in
a few minutes to twice its natural size. Salad oil is
the remedy relied on, and seldom known to fail. The
effect of anger on the common snake is marked. The
skin, if the creature is annoyed, becomes bristly and
colder; sometimes there is a strong snake-like smell
emitted. It is singular that the goat-sucker, or fern
owl, often stuffed when shot and preserved in glass
cases, does not keep; the bird looks draggled and
falling to pieces. So many of them are like this.
Some of the labouring people who work by the
numerous streamlets say that the wagtail dives, goes
right under water like a diver now and then—a circumstance I have not noticed myself. There is a
custom of serving up water-cress with roast fowl; it is
also sometimes boiled like a garden vegetable. Sometimes a man will take cider with his tea—a cup of tea
one side and a mug of cider on the other. The German
bands, who wander even into these extreme parts of

the country, always ask for cider, which they say reminds them of their own wines at home—like hock, or Rhenish. Though the junction of Barle and Exe is a long way from the sea (as the Exe winds), salmon come far up above that to the moors. Salmon-fishing is preserved, but poachers take them at night with gaffs. There are water-bailiffs, who keep a good look out, or think they do, but occasionally find heads of salmon nailed to their doors in derision. The missel-thrush is called the "holm-screech." The missel-thrushes, I know, have a difficulty to defend their young against crows; but last spring I found a jack-daw endeavouring to get at a missel-thrush's nest. The old birds were screeching loudly, and trying to drive the jackdaw away. The chaffinch appears to be called "wood-finch," at least the chaffinch answered nearest to the bird described to me as a "woodfinch." In another county it is called the piefinch.

One summer evening I was under a wood by the Exe. The sun had set, and from over the wooded hill above bars of golden and rosy cloud stretched out across the sky. The rooks came slowly home to roost, disappearing over the wood, and at the same time the herons approached in exactly the opposite direction, flying from Devon into Somerset, and starting out to feed as the rooks returned home. The first heron sailed on steadily at a great height, uttering a loud "caak, caak" at intervals. In a few minutes a second followed, and "caak, caak" sounded again over the river valley. The third was flying at a less height, and as he came into sight over the line of the wood he suddenly wheeled round, and, holding his immense

wings extended, dived as a rook will downwards
through the air. He twisted from side to side like a
coin partly spun round by the finger and thumb, as he
came down, rushing through the air head first. The
sound of his great vanes pressing and dividing the air
was plainly audible. He looked unable to manage his
descent; but at the right moment he recovered his
balance, and rose a little up into a tree on the summit,
drawing his long legs into the branches behind him.
The fourth heron fetched a wide circle, and so descended
into the wood; two more passed on over the valley—
altogether six herons in about a quarter of an hour.
They intended, no doubt, to wait in the trees till it
was dusky, and then to go down and fish in the river.
Herons are called cranes, and heronies are craneries.
A determined sportsman, who used to eat every heron
he could shoot in revenge for their ravages among the
trout, at last became suspicious, and, examining one,
found in it the remains of a rat and of a toad, after
which he did not eat any more. Another sportsman
found a heron in the very act of gulping down a good-
sized trout, which stuck in the gullet. He shot the
heron and got the trout, which was not at all injured,
only marked on each side where the beak had cut it.
The fish was cooked and eaten.

This summer evening the bars of golden and rosy
cloud gradually lost their bright colour, but retained
some purple in the vapour for a long time. If the red
sunset clouds turn black, the country people say it will
rain; if any other colour, it will be fine. The path
from the river led beside the now dusky moor, and
the curlew's weird whistle came out of the increasing

darkness. Wild as the curlew is in early summer
(when there are young birds), he will fly up within a
short distance of the wayfarer, whistling, and alight
on the burnt, barren surface of the moor. There he
stalks to and fro, grey and upright. He looks a large
bird so close. His head nods at each step, and every
now and then his long bill, curved like a sabre, takes
something from the ground. But he is not feeding, he
is watching you. He utters his strange, crying whistle
from time to time, which draws your attention from
the young birds.

By these rivers of the west otters are still numerous,
and are regularly hunted. Besides haunting the rivers,
they ascend the brooks, and even the smallest streamlets, and are often killed a long way from the larger
waters.

There are three things to be chiefly noticed in the
otter—first, the great width of the upper nostril;
secondly, the length and sharpness of the hold-fast
teeth; and, thirdly, the sturdiness and roundness of the
chest or barrel, expressive of singular strength. The
upper nostril is so broad that when the mouth is open
the lower jaw appears but a third of its width—a
mere narrow streak of jaw, dotted, however, with the
sharpest teeth. This distension of the upper jaw and
narrowness of the lower gives the impression of relent-
less ferocity. His teeth are somewhat catlike, and so
is his manner of biting. He forces his teeth to meet
through whatever he takes hold of, but then immediately repeats the bite somewhere else, not holding
what he has, but snapping again and again like a cat,
so that his bite is considered even worse than that of

the badger. Now and then, in the excitement of the
hunt, a man will put his hand into the hole occupied
by the otter to draw him out. If the huntsman sees
this there is some hard language used, for if the otter
chance to catch the hand, he might so crush and
mangle it that it would be useless for life. Nothing
annoys the huntsman more than anything of this kind.

The otter's short legs are deceptive; it does not
look as if a creature so low down could be very serious
to encounter or difficult to kill. His short legs are,
in fact, an addition to his strength, which is perhaps
greater than that of any other animal of proportionate
size. He weighs nearly as heavy as a fox, and is
even as hard to kill fairly. Unless speared, or knocked
heavily on the head, the otter-hounds can rarely kill
him in the water; when driven to land at last or to
a shallow he is often rather crushed and pressed to
death than anything else, and the skin sometimes
has not got a single toothmark in it. Not a single
hound has succeeded in biting through, but there
is a different story to tell on the other side. A
terrier has his jaw loose and it has to be bound up,
such a crushing bite has he had. There are torn
shoulders, necks, and limbs, and specks of blood on the
nostrils and coats of the other hounds. A full-grown
otter fights like a lion in the water; if he gets in a
hole under the bank where it is hollow, called a
"hover," he has to be thrust out with a pole. He
dives under the path of his enemies as they yelp in the
water, and as he goes attacks one from beneath, seizes
him by the leg, and drags him down, and almost
drowns him before he will let go. The air he is com-

pelled to emit from his lungs as he travels across to another retreat shows his course on the surface, and by the bubbles he is tracked as he goes deep below.

He tries up the stream, and finds at the place where a ledge of rocks crosses it eight or ten men armed with long staves standing waiting for him. If there was but one deep place at the side of the ledge of rocks he could beat them still and slip by, but the water is low for want of rain, and he is unable to do so. He turns and tries at the sides of the river lower down. Behind matted roots, and under the overhanging bank, with a rocky fragment at one side, he faces his pursuers. The hounds are snapped at as they approach in front. He cannot be struck with a staff from above because the bank covers him. Some one must wade across and strike him with a pole till he moves, or carry a terrier or two and pitch them in the hole, half above and half under water. Next he tries the other bank, then baffles all by doubling, till some one spies his nostril as he comes up to breathe. The rocky hill at hand resounds with the cries of the hounds, the sharp bark of the terriers, the orders of the huntsman, and the shouts of the others. There are ladies in the mead by the river's edge watching the hunt. Met in every direction, the otter swims down stream; there are no rocks there, he knows, but as he comes he finds a net stretched across. He cannot go down the river for the net, nor up it for the guarded ledge of rocks; he is enclosed in a pool without a chance of escape from it, and all he can do is to prolong the unequal contest to the last moment. Now he visits his former holes or " hovers " to be again found out; now he rests behind rocky fragments, now dives and doubles or eludes all for a minute by some turn. So long as his wind endures or he is not wounded he can stop in the water, and so long as he is in the water he can live. But by degrees he is encircled; some wade in and cut off his course; hounds stop him one way and men the other, till, finally forced to land or to the shallow, he is slain. His webbed feet are cut off and given as trophies to the ladies who are present. The skin varies in colour—sometimes a deep brown, sometimes fawn.

The otter is far wilder than the fox; for the fox a home is found and covers are kept for him, even though he makes free with the pheasants; but the otter has no home except the river and the rocky fastnesses beside it. No creature could be more absolutely wild, depending solely upon his own exertions for existence. Of olden time he was believed to be able to scent the fish in the water at a considerable distance, as a hound scents a fox, and to go straight to them. If he gets among a number he will kill many more than he needs. For this reason he has been driven by degrees from most of the rivers in the south where he used to be found, but still exists in Somerset and Devon. Not even in otter-hunting does he get the same fair play as the fox. No one strikes a fox or puts a net across his course. That, however, is necessary, but it is time that a strong protest was made against the extermination of the otter in rivers like the Thames, where he is treated as a venomous cobra might be on land. The truth is the otter is a most interesting animal and worth preservation, even at the cost of what he eats. There is a great difference between keeping the number of otters down by otter-hunting within reasonable limits and utterly exterminating them. Hunting the otter in Somerset is one thing, exterminating them in the Thames another, and I cannot but feel a sense of deep regret when I hear of fresh efforts towards this end. In the home counties, and, indeed, in many other counties, the list of wild creatures is already short enough, and is gradually decreasing, and the loss of the otter would be serious. This animal is one of the few perfectly wild creatures that have survived without any protection from the ancient forest days. Despite civilization, it still ventures, occasionally, within a few miles of London, and well inside that circle in which London takes its pleasure. It would be imagined that its occurrence so near the metropolis would be recorded with pride; instead of which, no sooner is the existence of an otter suspected than gun and trap are eagerly employed for its destruction.

I cannot but think that the people of London at large, if aware of these facts, would disapprove of the attempt to exterminate one of the most remarkable members of their fauna. They should look upon the inhabitants of the river as peculiarly their own. Some day, perhaps, they will take possession of the fauna and flora within a certain compass of their city. Every creature that could be kept alive within such a circle would be a gain, especially to the Thames, that well-head of the greatest city in the world. I marvel that they permit the least of birds to be shot upon its banks. Nothing at present is safe, not so much as a reedsparrow, not even the martins that hover over the stormy reaches. Where is the kingfisher?˙ Where are the water-fowl? Where soon will be the water-lilies? But if London extended its strong arm, how soon would every bush be full of bird-life, and the osier-beds and eyots the haunts of wild creatures! At this moment, it appears, so bitter is the enmity to the otter, that a reward is set on his head, and as much as two guineas is sometimes paid for the destruction of a full-grown one. Perhaps the following list of slaughter may call attention to the matter:—Three killed by Harlingham Weir in three years. On the 22nd of January, at East Molesey, opposite the Gallery at Hampton Court, in a field, a fine otter was shot, weighing twenty-six pounds, and measuring fifty-two inches. On the 26th of January, 1884, a small otter was killed at Thames Ditton. Both these were close to London from a sporting or natural history point of view. In February or March, 1884, an otter was killed at Cliefden Springs, Maidenhead; it measured fifty-one inches. Here, then, are six in a short period, and it is not a complete list; I have a distinct memory of one caught in a trap by Molesey Weir within the last two or three years, and then beaten to death with a spade.

THE WATER-COLLEY.

THE sweet grass was wet with dew as I walked
through a meadow in Somerset to the river. The
cuckoo sang, the pleasanter perhaps because his brief
time was nearly over, and all pleasant things seem to
have a deeper note as they draw towards an end.
Dew and sweet green grass were the more beautiful
because of the knowledge that the high hills around
were covered by sun-dried, wiry heather. River-side
mead, dew-laden grass, and sparkling stream were
like an oasis in the dry desert. They refreshed the
heart to look upon as water refreshes the weary. The
shadows were more marked and defined than they are
as day advances, the hues of the flowers brighter,
for the dew was to shadow and flower as if the
colours of the artist were not yet dry. Humble-bees
went down with caution into the long grass, not liking
to wet their wings. Butterflies and the brilliant
moths of a hot summer's morn alight on a dry heated
footpath till the dew is gone. A great rock rising
from the grass by the river's edge alone looked arid,
and its surface already heated, yet it also cast a cool
shadow. By a copse, two rabbits—the latest up of all
those which had sported during the night—stayed till

I came near, and then quietly moved in among the ferns and foxgloves.

In the narrowest part of the wood between the hedge and the river a corncrake called his loudest " crake, crake," incessantly. The corncrake or landrail is difficult even to see, so closely does he conceal himself in the tall grasses, and his call echoed and re-echoed deceives those who try to find him. Yet by great patience and watchful skilfulness the corncrake is sometimes caught by hand. If tracked, and if you can see him—the most difficult part—you can put your hand on him. Now and then a corncrake is caught in the same way by hand while sitting on her nest on the ground. It is not, however, as easy as it reads. Walking through the grass, and thinking of the dew and the beautiful morning sunshine, I scarcely noticed the quantity of cuckoo flowers, or cardamine, till presently it occurred to me that it was very late in the season for cuckoo-flowers ; and stooping I picked one, and in the act saw it was an orchis — the early purple. The meadow was coloured, or rather tinted, with the abundance of the orchis, palest of pale pink, dotted with red, the small narrow leaves sometimes with black spots. They grew in the pasture everywhere, from the river's side in the deep valley to the top of the hill by the wood.

As soon as the surface of the river was in sight I stood and watched, but no ripple or ring of wavelets appeared ; the trout were not feeding. The water was so low that the river consisted of a series of pools, connected by rapids descending over ledges of stones and rocky fragments. Illumined to the very bottom, every trout was visible, even those under the roots of trees and the hollow of the bank. A cast with the fly there was useless; the line would be seen; there was no ripple to hide it. As the trout, too, were in the pools, it might be concluded that those worth taking had fed, and only the lesser fish would be found in the eddies, where they are permitted by the larger fish to feed after they have finished. Experience and reason were all against the attempt, yet so delightful is the mere motion and delicate touch of the fly-line on the water that I could not but let myself enjoy that at least. The slender lancewood rod swayed, the line swished through the air, and the fly dropped a few inches too high up the rapid among the stones—I had meant it to fall farther across in the dark backwater at the foot of the fall. The swift rush of the current carried the fly instantly downwards, but not so quick as to escape a troutlet; he took it, and was landed immediately. But to destroy these under-sized fish was not sport, and as at that moment a water-colley passed I determined to let the trout alone, and observe his ways.

Colley means a blackbird; water-colley, the water-blackbird or water-ousel—called the dipper in the North. In districts where the bird is seldom seen it is occasionally shot and preserved as a white blackbird. But in flight and general appearance the water-colley is almost exactly like a starling with a white neck. His colour is not black or brown—it is a rusty, undecided brown, at a distance something the colour of a young starling, and he flies in a straight line, and yet clumsily, as a young starling does. His very cry, too, sounds immature, pettish, and unfinished, as if

K

from a throat not capable of a full note. There are usually two together, and they pass and re-pass all day as you fish, but if followed are not to be observed without care. I came on the colley too suddenly the first time, at a bend of the river; he was beneath the bank towards me, and flew out from under my feet, so that I did not see him till he was on the wing. Away he flew with a call like a young bird just tumbled out of its nest, following the curves of the stream. Presently I saw him through an alder bush which hid me; he was perched on a root of alder under the opposite bank. Worn away by the stream the dissolved earth had left the roots exposed, the colley was on one of them; in a moment he stepped on to the shore under the hollow, and was hidden behind the roots under a moss-grown stole. When he came out he saw me, and stopped feeding.

He bobbed himself up and down as he perched on the root in the oddest manner, bending his legs so that his body almost touched his perch, and rising again quickly, this repeated in quick succession as if curtsying. This motion with him is a sign of uncertainty—it shows suspicion; after he had bobbed to me ten times off he went. I found him next on a stone in the middle of the river; it stood up above the surface of a rapid connecting two pools. Like the trout, the colley always feeds at the rapids, and flies as they swim, from fall to fall. He was bobbing up and down, his legs bent, and his rusty brown body went up and down, but as I was hidden by a hedge he gained confidence, suspended his curtsying, and began to feed. First he looked all round the stone, and then stepped to another similar island in the midst of the rushing

water, pushing his head over the edge into it. Next
he stepped into the current, which, though shallow,
looked strong enough to sweep him away. The water
checked against him rose to the white mark on his
breast. He waded up the rapid, every now and then
thrusting his head completely under the water; sometimes he was up to his neck, sometimes not so deep; now
and then getting on a stone, searching right and left
as he climbed the cascade. The eddying water shot by
his slender legs, but he moved against it easily, and
soon ascended the waterfall. At the summit a second
colley flew past, and he rose and accompanied his friend.

Upon a ledge of rock I saw him once more, but there
was no hedge to hide me, and he would not feed; he
stood and curtsied, and at the moment of bobbing let
his wings too partly down, his tail drooping at the same
time. Calling in an injured tone, as if much annoyed,
he flew, swept round the meadow, and so to the river
behind me. His friend followed. On reaching the
river at a safe distance down, he skimmed along the
surface like a kingfisher. They find abundance of
insect life among the stones at the falls, and everywhere
in shallow water. Some accuse them of taking the
ova of trout, and they are shot at trout nurseries; but
it is doubtful if they are really guilty, nor can they do
any appreciable injury in an open stream, not being in
sufficient numbers. It is the birds and other creatures
peculiar to the water that render fly-fishing so
pleasant; were they all destroyed, and nothing left but
the mere fish, one might as well stand and fish in a
stone cattle-trough. I hope all true lovers of sport will
assist in preserving rather than in killing them.

NOTES ON LANDSCAPE PAINTING.

I.

THE earth has a way of absorbing things that are placed upon it, of drawing from them their stiff individuality of newness, and throwing over them something of her own antiquity. As the furrow smoothes and brightens the share, as the mist eats away the sharpness of the iron angles, so, in a larger manner, the machines sent forth to conquer the soil are conquered by it, become a part of it, and as natural as the old, old scythe and reaping-hook. Thus already the new agriculture has grown hoar.

The oldest of the modern implements is the threshing-machine, which is historic, for it was once the cause of rural war. There are yeomanry-men still living who remember how they rode about at night after the rioters, guided by the blazing bonfires kindled to burn the new-fangled things. Much blood —of John Barleycorn—was spilt in that campaign; and there is many a farmer yet hearty who recollects the ale-barrels being rolled up into the rickyards and there broached in cans and buckets, that the rebels, propitiated with plentiful liquor, might forbear to set fire to the ricks or sack the homestead. Such memories read strange to the present generation, proving thereby that the threshing-machine has already grown old. It is so accepted that the fields would seem to lack something if it were absent. It is as natural as the ricks : things grow old so soon in the fields.

On the fitful autumn breeze, with brown leaves whirling and grey grass rustling in the hedges, the hum of the fly-wheel sounds afar, travelling through the mist which hides the hills. Sometimes the ricks are in the open stubble, up the Down side, where the wind comes in a long, strong rush, like a tide, carrying away the smoke from the funnel in a sweeping trail; while the brown canvas, stretched as a screen, flaps and tears, and the folk at work can scarce hear each other speak, any more than you can by the side of the sea. Vast atmospheric curtains—what else can you call them ?—roll away, opening a view of the stage of hills a moment, and, closing again, reach from heaven to earth around. The dark sky thickens and lowers as if it were gathering thunder, as women glean wheat-ears in their laps. It is not thunder ; it is as if the wind grew solid and hurled itself—as a man might throw out his clenched fist—at the hill. The inclined plane of the mist-clouds again reflects a grey light, and, as if swept up by the fierce gale, a beam of sun-shine comes. You see it first long, as it is at an angle ; then overhead it shortens, and again lengthens after it has passed, somewhat like the spoke of a wheel. In the second of its presence a red handker-chief a woman wears on the ricks stands out, the brass on the engine glows, the water in the butt gleams, men's faces brighten, the cart-horse's coat looks glossy, the straw a pleasant yellow. It is gone, and lights up the backs of the sheep yonder as it runs up the hill swifter than a hare. Swish! The north wind darkens the sky, and the fly-wheel moans in the gloom; the wood-pigeons go a mile a minute on the wind, hardly using their wings; the brown woods below huddle together, rounding their shoulders to the blast; a great air-shadow, not mist, a shadow of thickness in the air looms behind a tiled roof in the valley. The vast profound is full of the rushing air.

These are days of autumn; but earlier than this, when the wheat that is now being threshed was ripe, the reaping-machine went round and round the field, beginning at the outside by the hedges. Red arms, not unlike a travelling windmill on a small scale, sweep the corn as it is cut and leave it spread on the ground. The bright red fans, the white jacket of the man driving, the brown and iron-grey horses, and yellow wheat are toned—melted together at their edges— with warm sunlight. The machine is lost in the corn, and nothing is visible but the colours, and the fact that it is the reaping, the time of harvest, dear to man these how many thousand years! There is nothing new in it; it is all old as the hills. The straw covers over the knives, the rims of the wheels sink into pimpernel, convolvulus, veronica; the dry earth powders them, and so all beneath is concealed. Above the sunlight (and once now and then the shadow of a tree) throws its mantle over, and, like the hand of an enchanter softly waving, surrounds it with a charm. So the cranks, and wheels, and knives, and mechanism do not exist—it was a machine in the workshop, but it is not a machine in the wheat-field. For the wheat-field you see is very, very old, and the air is of old time, and the shadow, the flowers, and the sunlight, and that which moves among them becomes of them. The solitary reaper alone in the great field goes round and round, the red fans striking beside him, alone with the sunlight, and the blue sky, and the distant hills; and he and his reaper are as much of the corn-field as the long-forgotten sickle or the reaping-hook.

The sharp rattle of the mowing-machine disturbs the corncrake in the meadow. Crake! crake! for many a long day since the grass began to grow fast in April till the cowslips flowered, and white parsley flourished like a thicket, blue scabious came up, and yonder the apple trees drop their bloom. Crake! crake! nearly day and night; but now the rattle begins, and the bird must take refuge in the corn. Like the reaper, the mowing-machine is buried under the swathe it cuts, and flowers fall over it—broad ox-eye daisies and red sorrel. Upon the hedge June roses bloom; blackbirds whistle in the oaks; now and again come the soft hollow notes of the cuckoo. Angles and wheels, cranks and cogs, where are they? They are lost; it is not these we see, but the flowers and the pollen on the grass. There is an odour of new-made hay; there is the song of birds, and the trees are beautiful.

As for the drill in spring-time, it is ancient indeed, and ancients follow it—aged men stepping after over the clods, and watching it as if it were a living thing, that the grains may fall each in its appointed place.

Their faces, their gait, nay, the very planting of their heavy shoes' stamp on the earth, are full of the importance of this matter. On this the year depends, and the harvest, and all our lives, that the sowing be accomplished in good order, as is meet. Therefore they are in earnest, and do not turn aside to gaze at strangers, like those do who hoe, being of no account. This is a serious matter, needing men of days, little of speech, but long of experience. So the heavy drill, with its hanging rows of funnels, travels across the field well tended, and there is not one who notes the deep azure of the March sky above the elms.

Still another step, tracing the seasons backwards, brings in the steam-plough. When the spotted arum leaves unfold on the bank, before the violets or the first celandine, while the " pussies " hang on the hazel, the engines roll into the field, pressing the earth into barred ruts. The massive wheels leave their imprint, the footsteps of steam, behind them. By the hedges they stand, one on either side, and they hold the field between them with their rope of iron. Like the claws of some pre-historic monster, the shares rout up the ground ; the solid ground is helpless before them ; they tear and rend it. One engine is under an oak, dark yet with leafless boughs, up through which the black. smoke rises ; the other overtops a low hedge, and is in full profile. By the panting, and the humming, and the clanking as the drum revolves, by the smoke hanging in the still air, by the trembling of the monster as it strains and tugs, by the sense of heat, and effort, and pent-up energy bubbling over in jets of steam that struggle through crevices somewhere, by

the straightened rope and the jerking of the plough
as it comes, you know how mighty is the power that
thus in narrow space works its will upon the earth.
Planted broadside, its four limbs—the massive wheels
—hold the ground like a wrestler drawing to him the
unwilling opponent. Humming, panting, trembling,
with stretched but irresistible muscles, the iron
creature conquers, and the plough approaches. All
the field for the minute seems concentrated in this
thing of power. There are acres and acres, scores of
acres around, but they are surface only. This is the
central spot: they are nothing, mere matter. This is
force—Thor in another form. If you are near you
cannot take your eyes off the sentient iron, the
wrestler straining. But now the plough has come
over, and the signal given reverses its way. The lazy
monotonous clanking as the drum unwinds on this
side, the rustling of the rope as it is dragged forth
over the clods, the quiet rotation of the fly-wheel—
these sounds let the excited thought down as the
rotating fly-wheel works off the maddened steam.
The combat over, you can look round.

It is the February summer that comes, and lasts a
week or so between the January frosts and the east
winds that rush through the thorns. Some little green
is even now visible along the mound where seed-leaves
are springing up. The sun is warm, and the still air
genial, the sky only dotted with a few white clouds.
Wood-pigeons are busy in the elms, where the ivy is
thick with ripe berries. There is a feeling of spring
and of growth; in a day or two we shall find violets;
and listen, how sweetly the larks are singing! Some

chase each other, and then hover fluttering above the hedge. The stubble, whitened by exposure to the weather, looks lighter in the sunshine, and the distant view is softened by haze. A water-tank approaches, and the cart-horse steps in the pride of strength. The carter's lad goes to look at the engine and to wonder at the uses of the gauge. All the brazen parts gleam in the bright sun, and the driver presses some waste against the piston now it works slowly, till it shines like polished silver. The red glow within, as the furnace-door is opened, lights up the lad's studious face beneath like sunset. A few brown leaves yet cling to one bough of the oak, and the rooks come over cawing happily in the unwonted warmth. The low hum and the monotonous clanking, the rustling of the wire rope, give a sense of quiet. Let us wander along the hedge, and look for signs of spring. This is to-day. To-morrow, if we come, the engines are half-hidden from afar by driving sleet and scattered snow-flakes fleeting aslant the field. Still sternly they labour in the cold and gloom. A third time you may find them, in September or bright October, with acorns dropping from the oaks, the distant sound of the gun, and perhaps a pheasant looking out from the corner. If the moon be full and bright they work on an hour or so by her light, and the vast shadows of the engines are thrown upon the stubble.

II.

Among the meadows the buttercups in spring are as innumerable as ever and as pleasant to look upon.

The petal of the buttercup has an enamel of gold; with the nail you may scrape it off, leaving still a yellow ground, but not reflecting the sunlight like the outer layer. From the centre the golden pollen covers the fingers with dust like that from the wing of a butterfly. In the bunches of grass and by the gateways the germander speedwell looks like tiny specks of blue stolen, like Prometheus' fire, from the summer sky. When the mowing-grass is ripe the heads of sorrel are so thick and close that at a little distance the surface seems as if sunset were always shining red upon it. From the spotted orchis leaves in April to the honeysuckle-clover in June, and the rose and the honeysuckle itself, the meadow has changed in nothing that delights the eye. The draining, indeed, has made it more comfortable to walk about on, and some of the rougher grasses have gone from the furrows, diminishing at the same time the number of cardamine flowers; but of these there are hundreds by the side of every tiny rivulet of water, and the aquatic grasses flourish in every ditch. The meadow-farmers, dairymen, have not grubbed many hedges—only a few, to enlarge the fields, too small before, by throwing two into one. So that hawthorn and blackthorn, ash and willow, with their varied hues of green in spring, briar and bramble, with blackberries and hips later on, are still there as in the old, old time. Bluebells, violets, cowslips—the same old favourite flowers—may be found on the mounds or sheltered near by. The meadow-farmers have dealt mercifully with the hedges, because they know that for shade in heat and shelter in storm the cattle resort to them. The hedges—yes, the hedges, the very synonym of Merry England—are yet there, and long may they remain. Without hedges England would not be England. Hedges, thick and high, and full of flowers, birds, and living creatures, of shade and flecks of sunshine dancing up and down the bark of the trees—I love their very thorns. You do not know how much there is in the hedges.

We have still the woods, with here and there a forest, the beauty of the hills, and the charm of winding brooks. I never see roads, or horses, men, or anything when I get beside a brook. There is the grass, and the wheat, the clouds, the delicious sky, and the wind, and the sunlight which falls on the heart like a song. It is the same, the very same, only I think it is brighter and more lovely now than it was twenty years ago.

Along the footpath we travel slowly ; you cannot walk fast very long in a footpath ; no matter how rapidly at first, you soon lessen your pace, and so country people always walk slowly. The stiles—how stupidly they are put together. For years and years every one who has passed them, as long as man can remember, has grumbled at them ; yet there they are still, with the elms reaching high above, and cows gazing over—cows that look so powerful, but so peacefully yield the way. They are a better shape than the cattle of the ancient time, less lanky, and with fewer corners ; the lines, to talk in yachtsman's language, are finer. Roan is a colour that contrasts well with meadows and hedges. The horses are finer, both cart-horse and nag. Approaching the farmsteads, there are hay-ricks, but there are fewer corn-ricks. Instead of the rows on

rows, like the conical huts of a savage town, there are
but a few, sometimes none. So many are built in the
fields and threshed there "to rights," as the bailiff
would say. It is not needful to have them near
home or keep them, now the threshing-machine has
stayed the flail and emptied the barns. Perhaps these
are the only two losses to those who look at things
and mete them with the eye—the corn-ricks and the
barns. The corn-ricks were very characteristic, but
even now you may see plenty if you look directly
after harvest. The barns are going by degrees,
passing out of the life of farming; let us hope that
some of them will be converted into silos, and so saved.

At the farmsteads themselves there are considerations for and against. On the one hand, the house
and the garden is much tidier, less uncouth; there
are flowers, such as geraniums, standard roses, those
that are favourites in towns; and the unsightly and
unhealthy middens and pools of muddy water have
disappeared from beside the gates. But the old
flowers and herbs are gone, or linger neglected in
corners, and somehow the gentle touch of time has
been effaced. The house has got a good deal away
from farming. It is on the farm, but disconnected.
It is a residence, not a farmhouse. Then you must
consider that it is more healthy, sweeter, and better
for those who live in it. From a little distance the
old effect is obtainable. One thing only I must
protest against, and that is the replacing of tiles with
slates. The old red tiles of the farmhouses are as
natural as leaves; they harmonize with the trees and the
hedges, the grass, the wheat, and the ricks. But slates

are wrong. In new houses, even farmhouses, it does not matter so much; the owners cannot be found fault with for using the advantages of modern times. On old houses where tiles were once, to put slates is an offence, nothing less. Every one who passes exclaims against it. Tiles tone down and become at home; they nestle together, and look as if you could be happily drowsy and slumber under them. They are to a house what leaves are to a tree, and leaves turn reddish or brown in the autumn. Upon the whole, with the exception of the slates—the hateful slates— the farmsteads are improved, for they have lost a great deal that was uncouth and even repulsive, which was slurred over in old pictures or omitted, but which was there.

The new cottages are ugly with all their ornamentation; their false gables, impossible porches, absurd windows, are distinctly repellent. They are an improvement in a sanitary sense, and we are all glad of that, but we cannot like the buildings. They are of no style or time; only one thing is certain about them—they are *not* English. Fortunately there are plenty of old cottages, hundreds of them (they show little or no sign of disappearing), and these can be chosen instead. The villages are to outward appearance much as they used to be, but the people are very different. In manners, conversation, and general tone there is a great change. It is, indeed, the people who have altered more than the surface of the country. Hard as the farmer may work, and plough and sow with engine and drill, the surface of the land does not much vary; but the farmer him-

self and the farmer's man are quite another race to
what they were. Perhaps it was from this fact that
the impression grew up that modern agriculture has
polished away all the distinctive characteristics of
the country. But it has not done so any more than
it has removed the hills. The truth is, as I have
endeavoured to explain, innovations so soon become
old in the fields. The ancient earth covers them with
her own hoar antiquity, and their newness disappears.
They have already become so much a part of the life
of the country that it seems as if they had always
been there, so easily do they fit in, so easily does the
eye accept them.

Intrinsically there is nothing used in modern
agriculture less symmetrical than what was previously
employed. The flails were the simplest of instruments,
and were always seen with the same accompaniment
—the interior of a barn. The threshing-machine is
certainly not less interesting; it works in the open
air, often with fine scenic surroundings, and the
number of people with it impart vivacity. In reaping
with the reaping-hook there were more men in the
wheat, but the reaping-machine is not without colour.
Scythes are not at all pleasant things; the mowing-
machine is at least no worse. As for the steam-plough,
it is very interesting to watch. All these fit in with
trees and hedges, fields and woods, as well, and in
some cases in a more striking manner than the old
instruments. The surface of the ground presents
more varied colours even than before, and the sunlight produces rich effects. Nor have all the ancient
aspects disappeared as supposed—quite the reverse.

In the next field to the steam-plough the old ploughs
drawn by horses may be seen at work, and barns still
stand, and the old houses. In hill districts oxen are
yet yoked to the plough, the scythe and reaping-hook
are often seen at work, and, in short, the old and the
new so shade and blend together that you can hardly
say where one begins and the other ends. That there
are many, very many things concerning agriculture and
country life whose disappearance is to be regretted I
have often pointed out, and having done so, I feel
that I can with the more strength affirm that in its
natural beauty the country is as lovely now as ever.

It is, I venture to think, a mistake on the part of some
who depict country scenes on canvas that they omit
these modern aspects, doubtless under the impression
that to admit them would impair the pastoral scene
intended to be conveyed. So many pictures and so
many illustrations seem to proceed upon the assumption that steam-plough and reaping-machine do not
exist, that the landscape contains nothing but what
it did a hundred years ago. These sketches are often
beautiful, but they lack the force of truth and reality.
Every one who has been fifty miles into the country,
if only by rail, knows while looking at them that they
are not real. You feel that there is something wanting, you do not know what. That something is the
hard, perhaps angular fact which at once makes the
sky above it appear likewise a fact. Why omit fifty
years from the picture? That is what it usually
means—fifty years left out; and somehow we feel
as we gaze that these fields and these skies are not
of our day. The actual fields, the actual machines,

the actual men and women (how differently dressed
to the conventional pictorial costumes!) would prepare
the mind to see and appreciate the colouring, the
design, the beauty—what, for lack of a better
expression, may be called the soul of the picture—far
more than forgotten, and nowadays even impossible
accessories. For our sympathy is not with them, but
with the things of our own time.

VILLAGE MINERS.

" RIGHT so, the hunter takes his pony which has been trained for the purpose, and stalks the deer behind him; the pony feeds towards the herd, so that they do not mind his approach, and when within a hundred yards, the hunter kneels down in the grass and fixes his iron rest or fork in the ground. He rests his Winchester rifle in the fork, and aims under the pony (which stands quite still), at his game. He generally kills one dead at the first shot, and wounds two or three more, firing rapidly after the first discharge so as to get as many shots as possible before the herd is out of range." So writes a friend in the wilds of Texas, adding that the hides fetch a few dollars. "Right so, departed Sir Launcelot." . . . "Right so, Sir Launcelot, his father, dressed his spear." . . . "Right so, he heard a voice that said;"—so runs the phrase in the "Mort d'Arthur," that ancient history of the Round Table, which was published nearly four hundred years ago. The coincidence of phrase indicates some resemblance in the circumstances, though so wide apart in time and distance. In England, in those old days, men lived in the woods and forests—out-of-doors—and were occupied with manual works.

They had no opportunities of polishing their discourse, or their literary compositions. At this hour, in remote parts of the great continent of America, the pioneers of modern civilization may be said to live amid mediæval surroundings. The vast forests and endless prairies give a romance to common things. Sometimes pathos and sometimes humour arises in the log-cabin, and when the history of these simple but deeply human incidents comes to be told in this country, we are moved by the strange piquancy of event and language. From the new sounds and scenes, these Anglo-Saxons hewing a way through pine and hemlock now, as their ancestors hewed a way into England, have added fresh words and phrases to our common tongue. These words are not slang, they are pure primeval language. They express the act, or the scene, or the circumstance, as exactly as if it was painted in sound. For instance, the word " crack " expresses the noise of a rifle ; say "crack," and you have the very sound; say " detonation," and it gives no ear-picture at all. Such a word is " ker-chunk." Imagine a huge log of timber falling from rock to rock, or a wounded opossum out of a tree, the word expresses the sound. There are scores of such examples, and it is these pure primitive words which put so much force into the narratives of American pathos and humour.

Now, the dwellers in our own villages and country places in their way make use of just such expressions, that is, of words which afford the ear a picture of the act or circumstance, hieroglyphs of sound, and often, both in language and character, exhibit a close parallelism with the Californian miners. Country people

say " fall " for autumn ; " fall " is the usual American
term for that season, and fall is most appropriate for
the downward curve of time, the descent of the leaf.
A slender slip of womanhood in the undeveloped period
is alluded to in the villages as a " slickit " of a girl.
" Slickit " means thin, slender, a piece that might be
whittled off a stick with a knife, not a shaving, for a
shaving curls, but a " slickit," a long thin slice. If
any one be' carving awkwardly with the left wrist
doubled under, the right arm angularly extended, and
the knife sawing at a joint, our village miners and country Californians call it " cack-" or " cag-handed." Cag-
handed is worse than back-handed ; it means awkward,
twisted, and clumsy. You may see many a cag-handed
person hacking at a fowl.

Hamlet folk are very apt to look a gift horse in
the mouth, and if any one should receive a present
not so large as expected, it would be contemptuously
described as a " footy " little thing. " Footy " pronounced with a sneering expression of countenance
conveys a sense of despicableness, even to those who
do not know its exact definition, which may be taken
as mean. Suppose a bunch of ripe nuts high up and
almost out of reach ; by dint of pressing into the
bushes, pulling at the bough, and straining on tiptoe,
you may succeed in "scraambing" it down. " Scraambing," or "scraambed," with a long accent on the aa,
indicates the action of stretching and pulling downwards. Though somewhat similar in sound, it has
no affinity with scramble ; people scramble for things
which have been thrown on the ground. In getting
through hedges the thorns are apt to "limm" one's

clothes, tearing a jagged hole in the coat. Country children are always "limming" their clothes to pieces; "limm," or "limb," expresses a ragged tear.

Recently, fashion set the example of ladies having their hair shorn as short as men. It is quite common to see young ladies, the backs of whose heads are polled, all the glory of hair gone, no plait, no twist, but all cut close and somewhat rough. If a village Californian were to see this he would say, " they got their hair hogged off." " Hogged " means cut off short so as to stand up like bristles. Ponies often have hogs' manes; all the horses in the Grecian sculpture have their manes hogged. In bitter winter weather the servants in the dairies who have much to do with buckets of water, and spend the morning in splashing— for dairies need much of that kind of thing—sometimes find that the drops have frozen as they walk, and discover that their aprons are fringed with " daglets," *i.e.* icicles. Thatched roofs are always hung with " daglets " in frost; thatch holds a certain amount of moisture, as of mist, and this drips during the day and so forms stalactites of ice, often a foot or more in length. " Clout " is a " dictionary word," a knock on the head, but it is pronounced differently here; they say a "clue" in the head. Stuttering and stammering each express well-known conditions of speech, but there is another not recognized in dictionary language. If a person has been made a butt of, laughed at, joked, and tormented till he hesitates and fumbles as it were with his words, he is said to be in a state of " hacka." " Hacka " is to have to think a minute before he can say what he wants to.

"Simmily" is a word of little interest, being evidently a mere provincialism and distortion of "seemingly," as "summat" of "something," or "somewhat," indifferently.

Occasionally a person is seized with a giggling fit, laughs on the least, or without any, provocation—a rather idiotic state—which he is quite conscious of but cannot stop. Persently some one will ask, "Have you found a wicker's nest?" which is a biting sarcasm, though the precise meaning seems uncertain, unless it bears some relation to mare's nest. Mares wicker, so do goats; giggling is wickering. The first work a boy does is to go out with a clapper, or his own strong voice, to scare birds from the corn all day; this we call bird-keeping, but the lads themselves, with an appreciation of the other side of the case, call it bird-starving. Forage is often used in a general sense of food, or in the more particular sense of green food, as clover, or vetches. Fodder, on the other hand, indicates dry food, such as hay; the labourers go twice a day in winter to fodder the cattle, that is, to carry them their hay. Many of these labourers before they start out to work, in their own words, "fodder" their boots. Some fine soft hay is pushed into the boots, forming a species of sock. Should either of them have a clumsy pair, they say his boots are like a seed-lip, which is a vessel like a basket used in sowing corn, and would be a very loose fit. They have not yet forgotten the ancient superstition about Easter Sunday, and the girls will not go out without a new ribbon at least; they must have something new on that day, if the merest trifle.

The backwoodsmen have found out many ways of curing cuts, wounds, bruises and injuries, rough methods, but effectual, and use the herbs and leaves much as their English forefathers did a century ago. For the most part in villages the knowledge and use of herbs has died out, and there are not many who resort to them. Elder-flower ointment, however, keeps its ground, and is, I think, still made for sale in the shops of towns. But the true country elder-flower ointment contains a little piece of adder's-tongue fern, which is believed to confer magical virtue. So curious a plant may naturally have had a mysterious value attached to it in old times. It is the presence of this touch of home-lore in the recipe which makes the product so different from the " ointment of the apothecary," manufactured by scale and weight and prosaic rule. Upon some roofs the houseleek still grows, though it is now often torn away as injurious. Where it grows it is usually on outhouses attached to the main building, sloping lean-tos. It does not present so glowing an appearance as the stonecrop, which now and then flourishes on houses, and looks like a brilliant golden cushion against the red tiles. The houseleek, however, is a singular plant, worthy of examination ; it has an old-world look, as if it had survived beyond its date into the nineteenth century. It hides in odd places and gables like a relic of witchcraft, and a black cat and an aged woman with a crutch-handled stick would be its appropriate owner. The houseleek is still used for the cure of wounds and cuts. A leaf —the leaves are rather like portions of the plant than mere leaves—is bruised to pulp, and the juice and some

of the pulp mixed with cream. They say it is effica-
cious. They call it "silgreen." In old English singreen means evergreen. Silgreen and singreen seem
close congeners. Possibly sil or sin may be translated
"through" as much as "ever," for the leaf of the plant
is thick, and green all through, if broken like a tough
cake. I think I would rather use it than the tobacco
juice which the mowers and reapers are now so fond
of applying to the cuts they frequently get. They
appear to have quite forsaken the ancient herbal
remedies, as the sickle-herb, knotted figwort, and so
on. Tobacco juice does not seem a nice thing for a
bleeding wound; probably it gets well rather in spite
of it than because of it.

If any one wanted a tonic in old farmhouses, it
used to be the custom, and till quite lately, to put
a nail in sherry, making an iron wine, which was
believed to be very restorative. Now, one of the
recent additions to the wine merchants' lists is a
sherry from Australia, Tintara, which is recommended
on account of its having been extracted from grapes
growing on an ironstone soil. So the old things come
up again in another form. There are scores of iron
tonics of various kinds sold in the shops; possibly the
nail in sherry was almost as good. Those who did not
care to purchase sherry, put their nail in cider. A few
odd names of plants may yet be heard among the
labourers, such as "loving-andrews" for the blue meadow
geranium; "loggerums" for the hard knapweed, and also
for the scabious; "Saturday night's pepper" for the
spurge, which grows wild in gardens; and there is a
weed called "good-neighbour," but as to which it is I

am ignorant. The spotted-leaf orchis flowers, which grow in moist and shady meads, lifting their purplish heads among the early spring grass, are called by the children "gran'fer goslings." To express extreme lack —as of money—they will say their purses are as bare as a toad is of feathers.

In these days it is the fashion to praise mattresses and to depreciate the feather-bed. Nothing so healthy as a mattress, nothing so good in every way. Mattresses are certainly cheaper, and there it ends. I maintain that no modern invention approaches the feather-bed. People try to persuade me to eat the coarsest part of flour—actually the rejected part—and to sleep on a mattress ; that is to say, to go back about twenty thousand years in civilization. But I decline. Having some acquaintance with wheat, I prefer the fine white flour, which is the very finest of all the products of the earth; having slept on all sorts of beds, sitting on a pole, lying on turf, leaning against a tree, and so forth, no one will ever persuade me that any couch is equal to a feather-bed. But should any desire a yet cheaper mattress than those advertised, I can put them in the way to obtain it. Among my hamlet Californians it is not unusual to find beds in use stuffed with the "hucks" of oats, *i.e.* the chaff. Like the backwoodsmen, they have to make shift with what they can get. Their ancestors steamed their arrows so as to soften the wood, when it was bound to a rigid rod and hung up in the chimney to dry perfectly straight. The modern cottager takes a stout stick and boils it in the pot till it becomes flexible. He then bends it into the

shape of a hook, ties it with string in that curve, and
suspends it in his chimney corner to dry crooked.
This crooked stick is the fagging-hook used to pull
the wheat towards the reaper with the left hand,
while he cuts it with the reap-hook in the right.

Suppose some one wavers and cannot make up his
mind. Now he will do this and now he will do that,
uncertain and unstable, putting his hand to the plough
and removing it again, my Californian at home would
call him "wivel-minded." "Wivelly" means undecided,
wavering, not to be depended on. It sounds like it.
If the labourer gets his clothes soaked, he says they
are "sobbled." The sound of boots or dress saturated
with rain very nearly approximates to sobbled. But
"gaamze" is the queerest word, perhaps, of all—it is to
smear as with grease. Beans are said to be "cherky,"
which means dry. Doubtless the obese old gentleman
in Boccaccio who was cured of his pains—the result
of luxurious living—by a diet which forced him to
devour beans for very hunger, did think them dry
and cherky. They have come up again now in the
shape of lentils, which are nothing but beans. It is
not generally known that Boccaccio was the inventor
of the bean cure. Cat's claws are notoriously apt to
scratch. Should a savage cat tear out a piece of flesh
from the hand, she is said to "dawk" it out. "Dawk"
expresses a ferocious dab and tear combined. A sharp
iron nail unseen might "dawk" the skin off an un-
wary hand. In ancient days when women quarrelled
and fought, they are said to have "dawked" fragments from each other's faces with their finger-nails.
Such incidents are now obsolete. It has often been

pointed out that many names of places are redupli-
cations. New layers of population, Saxon, Dane, or
Norman, added their words with the same meaning
to the former term. There is a hill called "Up-at-a-
Peak." "Up" itself signifies high, as in the endless
examples in which it forms the first syllable. "Peak,"
of course, is point. This is a modern reduplication,
not an archæological one.

If any one hacks and haws in speaking, it is called
"hum-dawing." Some very prominent persons of the
present day are much given to "hum-dawing," which
is often a species of conversational hedging. Are
"horse-stepple" and "stabbling" purely provincial,
or known in towns? "Stepple" is the mark or step
of a horse; "stabbling" is poaching up the turf or
ground from continual movement of feet, whether
human, equine, or otherwise. The ground near gateways in fields is often "stabbled" to such a degree
in wet weather as to appear impassable. A piece of
wood falling into water, gradually absorbs the liquid
into its pores, and swells. The same thing happens
in wet weather to gates and even doors; the wood
swells, so that if they fitted at all tightly before, they
can then scarcely be opened. Anything that swells
in this manner by absorption is said to "plim." A
sponge does not "plim;" it is not apparently larger
when full of water than previously, and it is still limp.
To "plim" up implies a certain amount of enlarge-
ment, and consequent tightness or firmness. Snow-
flakes are called "blossoms." The word snow-flake
is unknown. A big baby is always a thing to be
proud of, and you may hear an enthusiastic aunt

describing the weight and lumpiness of the youngster,
and winding up with the declaration, "He's a regular
nitch." A chump of wood, short, thick, and heavy,
is said to be a "nitch," but it seems gone out of use
a good deal for general weights, and to be chiefly used
in speaking of infants. There is a word of somewhat similar sound common among the fishermen of
the south coast. Towards the stern of a fishing
smack there is a stout upright post with a fork at
the top, into which fork the mast is lowered while
they are engaged with the nets at sea. It is called
the "mitch," or "match," but though I mention it
as similar in sound, I do not think it has any other
affinity.

Of old time, crab-apples were usually planted in
or near rickyards or elsewhere close to farmhouses.
The custom is now gone out; no crab-apples are
planted, and so in course of years there will be but
few. Crab-apple is not nearly so plentiful as anciently,
either in hedges or enclosures. The juice of the crab-
apple, varges, used to be valued as a cure for sprains.
The present generation can hardly understand that
there was a time when matches were not known. To
such a period must be traced the expression still
common in out-of-the-way places, of a "handful of
fire." A cottager who found her fire out would go
to a neighbour and bring home some live embers
to light up again. When the fire chances to be nearly
out, the expression is still heard both in cottages and
farmhouses, "There is hardly a handful of fire."
Such a mere handful is of course easily "douted." An
extinguisher "douts" a candle; the heel of a boot

"douts" a match thrown down. But the exact definition of "dout" is to smother, or extinguish by beating. In the days when wood fires were universal, as the wood burned, quantities of a fine white powder or ash collected, which at intervals, when the servant cleaned the hearth, was swept up into a corner. At night, if any embers remained glowing, a few shovel-fuls of this heap of white ash were thrown over them before retiring, and so the fire was "douted." To smother with such ashes precisely conveys the meaning of "dout." Incipient fires in grass, straw, or other material, are often beaten out as with bushes; this too is "douting." Stick your heels in the ground, arch your spine, and drag with all your might at a rope, and then you would be said to "scaut." Horses going uphill, or straining to draw a heavily laden waggon through a mud hole, "scaut" and tug. At football there is a good deal of "scauting." The axle of a wheelbarrow revolving without grease, and causing an ear-piercing sound, is said to be giving forth a "scrupeting" noise. What can be more explicit, and at the same time so aggravating, as to be told that you are a "mix-muddle"? A person who mixes up his commissions may feel a little abashed. A person who muddles his affairs may not be alto-gether proud of his achievements. But to be a mix-muddle, to both mix and muddle, to morally fumble without tact, and display a totally imbecile wander-ing; I shall get mixed myself if I try to describe such a state. Mixed in this sense is American too. Take a duster, dexterously swing it, and remove a fleck of dust from a table or books, and you will

understand the verb to "flirk," which is nearly the
same as to flick. "Pansherds" are "potsherds."

Here is a country recipe for discovering whether
a lover is faithful or not. Take a laurel leaf, scratch
his name on it, or the initials, and put it in the bosom
of the dress. If it turns brown, he is true ; if not,
he'll deceive you. The character of a girl, according
to the following couplets, is to be learned from the
colour of her eyes :—

> " Brown eyes, beauty,
>   Do your mother's duty.
> Blue eyes—pick-a-pie,
>   Lie a-bed and tell a lie.
> Grey eyes—greediness,
>   Gobble all the world up."

The interpretation is, that brown eyes indicate a
gentle and dutiful disposition. Blue eyes show three
guilty tendencies—to pick-a-pie, that is, to steal; to
lie a-bed, that is, to be idle ; and to tell a lie. As
for grey eyes, their selfish greediness and ambition
could not be contented with less than the whole
world. No one but a woman could have composed
this scandal on the sex. Sometimes the green lanes
are crossed by gates, over which the trees in the
hedges each side form a leafy arch. On the top bar
of such a gate, rustic lovers often write love messages
to their ladies, with a fragment of chalk. Unable
from some cause or other to keep the appointed
rendezvous, they leave a few explanatory words in
conspicuous white letters, so that the gate answers
the same purpose as the correspondence column in
the daily papers. When a gate is not available, they
thrust a stick in the ground near the footpath, split

the upper end, and place a piece of paper in it with the message.

The hamlet forge is not yet quite extinct, and the blacksmith's hammer sounds among the oaks. He frequently has to join two pieces of iron together, say to lengthen a rod. He places both ends in the fire, heats them to a certain point, and then presses the one against the other. By this simple means of touching they unite, the metal becomes one almost like a chemical union, and so complete is it, that, with a little polishing to remove the marks of fire, the join is not perceptible to an ordinary eye. This is the most perfect way of joining metal, and when accomplished, the pieces are said to be " butt-shut." The word has passed from the forge into conversation, and the expression is often heard, " That won't butt-shut." If any one be telling a tale, or giving an account of something of which his hearers are incredulous, they say it will not butt-shut—one part of the story will not agree and dovetail with the rest; there is a break in the continuity of the evidence, which does not unite and make one rod. Such a term is true miners' language. Indeed, the American backwoodsmen, miners, and so on, are really only English farmers and labourers transplanted to a freer and larger life.

MIND UNDER WATER.

THE thud, thud of a horse's hoof does not alarm fish. Basking in the sun under the bank, a jack or pike lying close to the surface of the water will remain unmoved, however heavy the sound may be. The vibrations reach the fish in several ways. There is what we should ourselves call the noise as conveyed by the air, and which in the case of a jack actually at the surface may be supposed to reach him direct. Next there is the vibration passing through the water, which is usually pronounced to be a good medium. Lastly, there is the bodily movement of the substance of the water. When the bank is hard and dry this latter amounts only to a slight shaking, but it frequently happens that the side of a brook or pond is soft, and "gives" under a heavy weight. Sometimes the edge is even pushed into the water, and the brook in a manner squeezed. You can see this when cattle walk by the margin; the grassy edge is pushed out, and in a minute way they may be said to contract the stream. It is in too small a degree to have the least apparent effect upon the water, but it is different with the sense of hearing, which is so delicate that the bodily movement thus caused may be reasonably believed to be very audible indeed to the jack. The wire fences which are now so much used round shrubberies and across parks give a very good illustration of the conveyance of sound. Strung tight by a spanner, the strands of twisted wire resemble a stringed instrument. If you place your hand on one of the wires and get a friend to strike it with his stick, say, thirty or forty yards away, you will distinctly feel it vibrate. If the ear is held close enough you will hear it, vibration and sound being practically convertible terms. To the basking jack three such wires extend, and when the cart-horse in the meadow puts down his heavy hoof he strikes them all at once. Yet, though fish are so sensitive to sound, the jack is not in the least alarmed, and there can be little doubt that he knows what it is. A whole herd of cattle feeding and walking about does not disturb him, but if the light step—light in comparison—of a man approach, away he goes. Poachers, therefore, unable to disguise their footsteps, endeavour to conceal them, and by moving slowly to avoid vibrating the earth, and through it the water.

In poaching, the intelligence of the man is backed against the intelligence of the fish or animal, and the poacher tries to get himself into the ways of the creature he means to snare. That is what really takes place as seen by us as lookers-on; to the poacher himself, in nine out of ten cases, it is merely an acquired knack learned from watching others, and improved by practice. But to us, as lookers-on, this is what occurs: the man fits himself to the ways of the creature, and for the time it becomes a struggle between them. It

M

is the same with the Red Indians, and the white trappers and hunters in wild regions, who depend much more on their knowledge of the ways and habits of the fur-bearing animals than upon their skill with the rifle. A man may be an excellent shot with gun or rifle, and yet be quite incapable of coping on comparatively equal terms with wild creatures. He is a sportsman, depending on skill, quick sight, and ready hand—not a hunter. Perhaps the nearest approach to it in legitimate English sport is in fly-fishing and salmon fishing, when the sportsman relies upon his own unassisted efforts. Deer-stalking, where the sportsman has to reckon on the wind, and its curious twists and turns in valleys and round rocks, would be a very near approach to it did the stalker stalk alone. But all this work is usually done for him by an attendant, a native Highlander; and this man really does pit his intelligence against that of the stag. The Highlander actually is a Red Indian, or hunter, and in this sense struggles with the wild animal. The poacher is the hunter on illegitimate ground, and with arts which it has been mutually agreed shall not be employed.

Considered in this sense it is interesting to observe to what extent the intelligence even of a fish reaches —and I think upon reflection it will be found that the fish is as clever as any creature could be in its position. I deny altogether that the cold-blooded fish—looked on with contempt so far as its intellectual powers are concerned—is stupid, or slow to learn. On the contrary, fish are remarkably quick, not only under natural conditions, but quick at accommodating themselves to altered circumstances which they could not foresee, and the knowledge how to meet which could not have been inherited. The basking jack is not alarmed at the cart-horse's hoofs, but remains quiet, let them come down with ever so heavy a thud. He has observed that these vibrations never cause him any injury. He hears them at all periods of the day and night, often with long intervals of silence and with every possible variation. Never once has the sound been followed by injury or by anything to disturb his peace. So the rooks have observed that passing trains are harmless, and will perch on the telegraph wires or poles over the steam of the roaring locomotive. Observation has given them confidence. Thunder of wheels and immense weight in motion, the open furnace and glaring light, the faces at the long tier of windows—all these terrors do not ruffle a feather. A little boy with a wooden clapper can set a flock in retreat immediately. Now the rooks could not have acquired this confidence in the course of innumerable generations; it is not hereditary; it is purely what we understand by intelligence. Why are the rooks afraid of the little boy with the clapper ? Because they have noticed his hostile intent. Why is the basking jack off the instant he hears the light step of a man ?

He has observed that after this step there have often followed attempts to injure him; a stone has been flung at him, a long pole thrust into the water; he has been shot at, or felt the pinch of a wire. He remembers this, and does not wait for the attempt to be repeated, but puts himself into safety. If he did not realize that it was a man—and a possible enemy—he would not trouble. The object consequently of the tricks of the poacher is to obliterate himself. If you can contrive to so move, and to so conduct yourself that the fish shall not recognize you as his enemy, you can do much as you please with him, and in varying degrees it is the same with animals. Think a moment by what tokens a fish recognizes a man. First, his light, and, compared with other animals, brisk step—a two-step instead of a four-step, remember; two feet, not four hoofs. There is a difference at once in the rhythm of the noise. Four hoofs can by no possibility produce the same sound, or succession of sounds, as is made even by four feet—that is, by two men. The beats are not the same. Secondly, by his motions, and especially the brisk motions of the arms. Thirdly, by this briskness itself; for most animals, except man, move with a slow motion—paradox as it may seem—even when they are going along fast. With them it is usually repose in action. Fourthly—and this is rather curious—experience seems to show that fish, and animals and birds certainly, recognize man by his hat or cap, to which they have a species of superstitious dislike.

Hats are generally of a different hue to the rest of the suit, for one thing; and it was noted, a century ago, that wild creatures have a particular objection to a black hat. A covering to the head at all is so opposite to their own ideas that it arouses suspicion, for we must remember that animals look on our clothes as our skin. To have a black skin over the

hair of the head is somewhat odd. By all these signs
a fish knows a man immediately, and as certainly as
any creature moving on land would know him. There
is no instinctive or hereditary fear of man at all—it
is acquired by observation (which a thousand facts
demonstrate); so that we are quite justified in
believing that a fish really does notice some or all of
these attributes of its enemy. What the poacher or
wild hunter has to do is to conceal these attributes.
To hide the two-step, he walks as slowly as possible,
not putting the foot down hard, but feeling the ground
first, and gradually pressing it. In this way progress
may be made without vibration. The earth is not
shaken, and does not communicate the sound to the
water. This will bring him to the verge of the place
where the fish is basking.

Very probably not only fish, but animals and some
birds hear as much by the vibration of the earth as by
the sound travelling in the atmosphere, and depend
as much upon their immediate perception of the
slightest tremor of the earth as upon recognition by
the ear in the manner familiar to ourselves. When
rabbits, for instance, are out feeding in the grass, it is
often possible to get quite close to them by walking in
this way, extremely slowly, and carefully placing the
foot by slow degrees upon the ground. The earth is
then merely pressed, and not stepped upon at all, so
that there is no jar. By doing this I have often
moved up within gunshot of rabbits without the least
aid from cover. Once now and then I have walked
across a field straight at them. Something, however,
depends on the direction of the wind, for then the

question of scent comes in. To some degree it is the
same with hares. It is certainly the case with birds,
as wood-pigeons, a flock of them, will remain feeding
only just the other side of the hedge; but, if you
stamp the earth, will rise instantly. So will rooks,
though they will not fly far if you are not armed.
Partridges certainly secure themselves by their attention to the faint tremor of the ground. Pheasants
do so too, and make off, running through the underwood long before any one is in sight. The most
sensitive are landrails, and it is difficult to get near
them, for this reason. Though the mowing-grass must
conceal an approaching person from them as it conceals them from him, these birds change their positions,
no matter how quietly he walks. Let him be as cunning as he will, and think to cut off corners and cross
the landrail's retreat, the bird baffles him nine times
in ten. That it is advised of the direction the pursuer
takes by the vibration of the surface is at least probable. Other birds sit, and hope to escape by remaining still, till they detect the tremor coming direct
towards them, when they rise.

Rain and dry weather change the susceptibility of
the surface to vibrate, and may sometimes in part
account for the wildness or apparent tameness of birds
and animals. Should any one doubt the existence of
such tremors, he has only to lie on the ground with
his ear near the surface; but, being unused to the experiment, he will at first only notice the heavier sounds,
as of a waggon or a cart-horse. In recent experiments
with most delicate instruments devised to show the
cosmic vibration of the earth, the movements com-

municated to it by the tides, or by the "pull" of the
sun and moon, it has been found almost impossible as
yet to carry out the object, so greatly are these movements obscured by the ceaseless and inexplicable
vibrations of the solid earth. There is nothing un-
reasonable in the supposition that, if an instrument
can be constructed to show these, the ears of animals
and birds—living organisms, and not iron and steel—
should be able to discover the tremors of the surface.

The wild hunter can still further check or altogether
prevent observation by moving on hands and knees,
when his weight is widely distributed. In the particular instance of a fish he endeavours to come to the
margin of the water at the rear of the fish, whose eyes
are so placed that it can see best in front. When he
has arrived at the margin, and has to rear himself up,
if from hands and knees, or, if already upright, when
he commences his work, he tries to conceal his arms,
or, rather, to minimize their peculiar appearance as
much as practicable by keeping them close to his sides.
All this time I am supposing that you are looking
at the poacher from the fish. To a fish or any wild
animal the arms of a man are suspicious. No other
creature that they know possesses these singular
appurtenances, which move in almost any direction,
and yet have nothing to do with locomotion. You
may be sure that this great difference in the
anatomical construction of a man is recognized by all
wild animals once they are compelled for their own
safety to observe him. Arms are so entirely opposite
to all the varieties of limb possessed by the varieties
of living creatures.

Can you put yourselves in the position of either of these creatures—moving on all-fours, on wings, or by the aid of a membraneous tail and fins, and without arms, and imagine how strange the arms of a man must look ? Suppose yourself with your arms tucked to your sides under the fur of an animal ; something of the idea may be gathered by putting on a cloak without sleeves or armholes. At once it will be apparent how helpless all creatures are in comparison with man. It is true that apes are an exception ; yet their arms are also legs, and they are deficient in the power of the thumb. Man may be defined as an animal with arms. While the creatures of the field or the water have no cause to fear him they do not observe him, but the moment they learn that he is bent on their destruction they watch him narrowly, and his arms are, above all, the part which alarms them. To them these limbs are men's weapons— his tusks, and tusks which strike and wound afar. From these proceed an invisible force which can destroy where it would seem the intervening distance alone would afford safety. The sharp shot, the keen hook, the lacerating wire, the spear—everything which kills or wounds, comes in some manner or other from the arms, down to the stone or the primitive knob-kerrie. Consequently animals, birds, and fishes not only in our own, but in the wildest countries, have learned to watch and to dread man's arms. He raises his arms, and in an instant there shoots forth a bright flash of flame, and before the swift wings can beat the air again the partridge is dashed to the ground.

So long as a gun is carried under the arm—that is,

with the arms close to the sides—many birds will let the sportsman approach. Rabbits will do the same. Rabbits have one advantage (and perhaps only one) : being numerous and feeding out by daylight, all kinds of experiments can be tried on them, while hares are not so easily managed. Suppose a rabbit feeding, and any one with a gun creeping up beside the hedge, while the gun is kept down and the arms down the rabbit remains still; the instant the arms are lifted to point the gun, up he sits, or off he goes. You have only to point your arm at a rook, without any gun, to frighten him. Bird-keepers instinctively raise their arms above their heads, when shouting, to startle birds. Every creature that has ever watched man knows that his arms are dangerous. The poacher or wild hunter has to conceal his arms by reducing their movements to a minimum, and by conducting those movements as slowly as possible.

To thoroughly appreciate the importance which animals of all kinds put on the motions of the upper limbs, and to put one's self quite in their position, one has only to recall to mind the well-known trick of the Australian bushrangers. "Bail up!" is their order when they suddenly produce their revolvers; "Bail up!" they shout to the clerks of the bank they are about to sack, to the inmates of a house, or to the travellers they meet on the road. "Hold your arms above your head" is the meaning; and, if it is not immediately obeyed, they fire. They know that every man has a pistol in his pocket or belt; but he cannot use it if compelled to keep his arms high over his head. One or more of the band keep a sharp look-out

on the upheld arms while the rest plunder; and, if any
are lowered—bang! Like the animals, they know the
extreme danger to be apprehended from movements
of the human arms. So long as the human arms are
"bailed" (though in this case in an opposite direction,
i.e. held down), animals are not afraid. Could they
make us "bail up," we should be helpless to injure
them. Moving his arms as gently as possible, with the
elbows close to his sides, the poacher proceeds to slowly
push his rod and wire loop towards the basking jack.
If he were going to shoot partridges at roost on the
ground, he would raise his gun in an equally slow and
careful manner. As a partridge is a small bird, and
stands at about a shilling in the poacher's catalogue,
he does not care to risk a shot at one, but likes to
get several at once. This he can do in the spring,
when the birds have paired and remain so near together, and again in the latter part of the summer, when
the coveys are large, not having yet been much broken
up by the sportsmen. These large coveys, having
enjoyed an immunity from disturbance all through the
summer, wandering at their own will among clover
and corn, are not at all difficult to approach, and a shot
at them through a gap in a hedge will often bring
down four or five. Later on the poacher takes them
at roost. They roost on the ground in a circle, heads
outwards, much in the same position as the eggs of a
lapwing. The spot is marked; and at night, having
crept up near enough, the poacher fires at the spot
itself rather than at the birds, with a gun loaded with a
moderate charge of powder, but a large quantity of shot,
that it may spread wide. On moderately light nights

he can succeed at this game. It is in raising the arms
to point the gun that the risk of alarming the birds
has to be met; and so with a hare sitting in a form in
daytime. Lift your arms suddenly, and away she
goes; keep your arms still, and close to your side, and
she will sit till you have crept up actually to her very
side, and can pounce on her if you choose.

Sometimes, where fish have not been disturbed by
poachers, or loafers throwing stones and otherwise
annoying them, they will not heed a passer-by, whose
gentle walk or saunter does not affright them with
brisk motion, especially if the saunterer, on espying
them, in no degree alters his pace or changes his
manner. That wild creatures immediately detect a
change of manner, and therefore of mood, any one may
demonstrate for himself. They are as quick to see it
as the dog, who is always with his master, and knows
by the very way he puts a book on the table what
temper he is in. When a book goes with a bang on
the table the dog creeps under it. Wild creatures, too,
catch their manners from man. Walk along a lane
with your hands in your pockets, and you will see
twice as much of the birds and animals, because they
will not set themselves to steadfastly watch you. A
quick movement sets wings quickly beating. I have
noticed that even horses in stables do not like visitors
with jerky, brisk, angular ways of moving. A stranger
entering in a quiet, easy manner is not very objection-
able, but if he comes in in a bustling, citizen-like style,
it is quite probable that one or other horse will show a
wicked white corner in his eye. It roughs them up
the wrong way. Especially all wild creatures dislike

the shuffling, mincing step so common in towns. That alone will disturb everything. Indeed, I have often thought that a good and successful wild hunter—like the backwoodsman, or the sportsman in African bush or Indian jungle—is really made as much by his feet as his eyes or hands. Unconsciously he feels with his feet; they come to know the exact time to move, whether a long or short stride be desirable, and where to put down, not to rustle or cause a cracking sound, and accommodate themselves to the slope of the ground, touching it and holding it like hands. A great many people seem to have no feet; they have boots, but no feet. They stamp or clump, or swing their boots along and knock the ground at every step; this matters not in most callings, but if a man wish to become what I have called a wild hunter, he must let his feet learn. He must walk with hands in his boots. Now and then a person walks like this naturally, and he will come in and tell you that he has seen a fish basking, a partridge, a hare, or what not, when another never gets near anything. This is where they have not been much disturbed by loafers, who are worse than poachers.

As a rule, poachers are intermittent in their action, and they do not want to disturb the game, as it makes it wild and interferes with their profits. Loafers are not intermittent — they are always about, often in gangs, and destroy others' sport without having any themselves. Near large towns there are places where the fish have to be protected with hurdles thrown across the stream on poles, that the stones and brickbats hurled by every rascal passing may not make their very life a burden. A rural poacher is infinitely preferable. The difference in the ways of fish when they have been much disturbed and when they have been let alone is at once discerned. No sooner do you approach a fish who has been much annoyed and driven than he strikes, and a quick-rotating curl on the surface shows with what vehemence his tail was forced against it. In other places, if a fish perceives you, he gives himself so slight a propulsion that the curl hardly rises, and you can see him gliding slowly into the deeper or overshadowed water. If in terror he would go so quickly as to be almost invisible. In places where the fish have been much disturbed the poacher, or any one who desires to watch their habits, has to move as slowly as the hands of a clock, and even then they will scarcely bear the very sight of a man, sometimes not at all. The least briskness of movement would send them into the depths out of sight. Cattle, to whom they are accustomed, walk slowly, and so do horses left to themselves in the meads by water. The slowest man walking past has quicker, perhaps because shorter, movements than those of cattle and horses, so that, even when bushes intervene and conceal his form, his very ways often proclaim him.

Most people will only grant a moderate degree of intelligence to fish, linking coldness of blood to narrowness of intellect, and convinced that there can be but little brain in so small a compass as its head. That the jack can compete with the dog, of course, is out of the question; but I am by no means prepared to admit that fish are so devoid of sense as supposed. Not long

since an experiment was tried with a jack, an account
of which appeared in the papers. The jack was in a
tank, and after awhile the tank was partly divided by
inserting a plate of glass. He was then hunted round,
and notes taken of the number of times he bumped his
head against the plate of glass, and how long it took
him to learn that there was something to obstruct his
path. Further statistics were kept as to the length of
his memory when he had learnt the existence of the
glass—that is, to see if he would recollect it several
days afterwards. The fish was some time learning the
position of the glass; and then, if much alarmed, he
would forget its position and dash against it. But he
did learn it, and retained his memory some while. It
seems to me that this was a very hard and unfair test.
The jack had to acquire the idea of something transparent, and yet hard as wood. A moment's thought
will show how exactly opposite the qualities of glass
are to anything either this particular fish or his
ancestors could have met with—no hereditary intelligence to aid him, no experience bearing, however
slightly, upon the subject.

Accustomed all his life to tranparent water, he
had also been accustomed to find it liquid, and easily
parted. Put suddenly face to face with the transparent material which repelled him, what was he to
think? Much the same effect would be produced if
you or I, having been accustomed, of course, all our
lives, to the fluidity of air, which opens for our
passage, were opposed by a solid block of transparent
atmosphere. Imagine any one running for a train,
and striking his head with all his might against such

a block. He would rise, shake himself together, and
endeavour to pursue his journey, and be again repelled. More than likely he would try three times
before he became convinced that it really was something in the air itself which stopped him. Then he
would thrust with his stick and feel, more and more
astounded every moment, and scarcely able to believe
his own senses. During the day, otherwise engaged,
he would argue himself into the view that he had
made a mistake, and determine to try again, though
more cautiously. But so strong is habit that if a
cause for alarm arose, and he started running, he
might quite probably go with tremendous force up to
the solid block of transparent air, to be hurled back
as the jack was.

These are no mere suppositions, for quite recently
I heard of a case which nearly parallels the conduct
of the jack. A messenger was despatched by rail
to a shop for certain articles, and was desired to
return by a certain time. The parcel was made up,
the man took it, heard an engine whistle, turned to
run, and in his haste dashed himself right through
a plate-glass window into the street. He narrowly
escaped decapitation, as the great pieces of glass fell
like the knife of a guillotine. Cases of people injuring
themselves by walking against plate-glass are by no
means uncommon; when the mind is preoccupied it
takes much the same place as the plate of glass in
the water and the jack. Authorities on mythology
state that some Oriental nations had not arrived at
the conception of a fluid heaven—of free space; they
thought the sky was solid, like a roof. The fish was

very much in the same position. The reason why fish
swim round and round in tanks, and do not beat themselves against the glass walls, is evidently because
they can see where the water ends. A distinction is
apparent between it and the air outside; but when the
plate of glass was put inside the tank the jack saw
water beyond it, or through it. I never see a fish in a
tank without remembering this experiment and the
long train of reflections it gives rise to. To take a fish
from his native brook, and to place him suddenly in
the midst of such, to him, inconceivable conditions, is
almost like watching the actual creation of mind. His
mind has to be created anew to meet it, and that it did
ultimately meet the conditions shows that even the
fish—the cold-blooded, the narrow-brained—is not
confined to the grooves of hereditary knowledge alone,
but is capable of wider and novel efforts. I thought
the jack came out very well indeed from the trial, and
I have mentioned the matter lest some should think I
have attributed too much intelligence to fish.

Other creatures besides fish are puzzled by glass.
One day I observed a robin trying to get in at the
fanlight of a hall door. Repeatedly he struck himself
against it, beat it with his wings, and struggled to get
through the pane. Possibly there was a spider inside
which tempted him; but allowing that temptation, it
was remarkable that the robin should so strive in vain.
Always about houses, he must have had experience of
the properties of glass, and yet forgot it so soon. His
ancestors for many generations must have had experience of glass, still it did not prevent him making
many trials. The slowness of the jack to learn the

impenetrable nature of the glass plate and its position is not the least indication of lack of intelligence. In daily life we constantly see people do things they have observed injure them, and yet, in spite of experience, go and do the same again.

The glass experiment proves to me that the jack, like all other creatures, really has a latent power of intelligence beyond that brought into play by the usual circumstances of existence. Consider the conditions under which the jack exists—the jack we have been approaching so carefully. His limits are the brook, the ponds it feeds, and the ditches that enter it. He can only move a short distance up the stream because there is a high hatch, nor can he go far down because of a mill; if he could, the conditions would be much the same; but, as a matter of fact, the space he has at his command is not much. The running water, the green flags, the lesser fishes, the water-rats, the horses and cattle on the bank—these are about all the things that he is likely to be interested in. Of these only the water, the lesser fishes, the flags, and the bottom or sides of the brook, are actually in his touch and complete understanding. As he is unable to live out of water, the horse on the bank, in whose very shadow he sometimes lies, might be a mile away for aught it concerns him. By no possible means can he discover anything about it. The horse may be itself nothing more than a shadow, unless in a shallow place he steps in and splashes. Night and day he knows, the cool night, and the sunbeams in which he basks; but he has no way of ascertaining the nature of anything outside the

N

water. Centuries spent in such conditions could add
but little to his experience.

Does he hear the stream running past him? Do
the particles of water, as they brush his sides and
fins, cause a sound, as the wind by us? While he
lurks beneath a weed in the still pool, suddenly a
shoal of roach rush by with a sound like a flock of
birds whose wings beat the air. The smooth surface
of the still water appears to cover an utter silence,
but probably to the fish there are ceaseless sounds.
Water-fowl feeding in the weedy corners, whose legs
depend down into the water and disturb it; water-
rats diving and running along the bottom; water-
beetles moving about; eels in the mud; the lower
parts of flags and aquatic grasses swinging as the
breeze ruffles their tips; the thud, thud of a horse's
hoofs, and now and then the more distant roll of
a hay-laden waggon. And thunder — how does
thunder sound under the surface? It seems reasonable to suppose that fish possess a wide gamut
of hearing since their other senses are necessarily
somewhat curtailed, and that they are peculiarly
sensitive to vibratory movements is certain from the
destruction a charge of dynamite causes if exploded
under water. Even in the deep sea the discharge of a
torpedo will kill thousands of herrings. They are as
it were killed by noise. So that there are grounds
for thinking that my quiet jack in the pool, under the
bank of the brook, is most keenly alive by his sense
of hearing to things that are proceeding both out and
in the water. More especially, no doubt, of things in
the water itself. With all this specialized power of

hearing he is still circumscribed and limited to the groove of the brook. The birds fly from field to field, from valley to mountain, and across the sea. Their experience extends to whole countries, and their opportunities are constant. How much more fortunate in this respect than the jack! A small display of intelligence by the fish is equivalent to a large display by the bird.

When the jack has been much disturbed no one can do more than obtain a view of him, however skilfully he may conceal himself. The least sign of further proceedings will send the jack away; sometimes the mere appearance of the human form is sufficient. If less suspicious, the rod with the wire attached—or if you wish to make experiments, the rod without the wire—can be placed in the water, and moved how you choose.

SPORT AND SCIENCE.

KINGFISHER CORNER was the first place I made for when, as a lad, I started from home with my gun. The dew of September lies long on the grass, and by the gateway I often noticed wasps that had spent the night in the bunches, numbed and chilled, crawling up the blades bent into an arch by the weight of the drops. Thence they got on the gate, where, too, the flies congregated at that time in the morning; for while it was still cool at the surface of the ground, the dry wood soon absorbed the heat of the sun. This warmth brought them to life again, and after getting well charged with it, the insects flew off to any apples they could discover. These heavy dews, as the summer declines, keep the grass fresh and green, and maintain the leaves on hedge and tree; yet they do not reach the earth, which remains dry. It is a different dew to the spring dew, or acts in another manner: the spring dews moisten the earth, and from the arable lands as the sun shines forth you may see the vapour rise and drift along the surface; like the smoke of a gun on a damp day. The mottled geometrical giant spiders find their webs thick with this September dew, which seems as if a little unctuous. Stepping through the

gateway with the morning sun behind me, I saw at
each step a fresh circle of dewdrops gleam, some ruby,
some emerald, some brightly white, at the same
distance in front. The angle of refraction advanced
as I moved; there was a point at which the dewdrop
shot back a brilliant ray, and then became invisible,
or appeared a mere drop of dull water.

By moonlight there is thus formed a semicircle of
light on the grass, which continually moves before you;
it is a halo on the grass-tips. I noticed this as a boy,
and tried all sorts of experiments respecting it, but never
met with any mention of it in books till quite lately,
in Benvenuto Cellini's "Autobiography." He says,
"There appeared a resplendent light over my head,
which has displayed itself conspicuously to all I have
thought proper to show it to, but those were very few.
This shining light is to be seen in the morning over *my
shadow* till two o'clock in the afternoon, and it appears
to the greatest advantage when the *grass is moist with
dew;* it is likewise visible in the evening at sunset.
This phenomenon I took notice of in Paris, because
the air is exceedingly clear in that climate, so that I
could distinguish it there much plainer than in Italy,
where mists are much more frequent; but I can still
see it even here, and show it to others, though not to
the same advantage as in France." Benvenuto thought
this one of the most extraordinary things that had
happened to him; and records it after a wonderful
dream, as if it, too, were supernatural. It is, however,
possible that some eyes are so constituted as not to be
able to see this phenomenon in their own case; at
least, I have sometimes tried in vain to get other

people to see it. I should not have noticed it had I not been about at all hours with my gun as a boy. It is much more visible by moonlight, when the rabbits' white tails go dot, dot, lightly over the grass, and you are just as likely to shoot at their shadows as at their bodies. As the scythe of the mower mows a swathe before him, so the semicircle of light moves in front over the dew, and the grass appears another tint, as it does after a roller has passed.

In a scientific publication not long since, a letter was published describing what the writer supposed was indeed something extraordinary. He had seen a fragment of rainbow—a square piece, as it were—by itself in the sky, some distance to one side of the sun. In provincial papers such letters may often be found, and even, until lately, in papers issued in London; now with accurate accounts of an ordinary halo about the sun, now with a description of a prismatic cloud round the moon, and one day some one discovered that there were two currents of air, as the clouds went in two directions. Now, it is clear enough that none of these writers had ever been out with a gun or a rod; I mean out all day, and out in the full sense of the phrase. They had read books of science; from their language they were thoroughly educated, and felt a deep interest in natural phenomena. Yet what a marvel was here made out of the commonest incidents of the sky! Halos about the sun happen continually; the prismatic band or cloud about the moon is common; so is the detached rainbow; as for the two currents of air, the clouds often travel in three directions, occasionally in four. These incidents are no more surprising to a sportsman than the sunset. I saw them, as a boy, almost day by day, and recorded the meteors in the evening. It seems to me that I used to see scores of meteors of various degrees of brightness. Once the path, the woods, the fields, and the distant hills were lit as if with a gigantic electric light; I was so interested in tracing the well-known scene so suddenly made apparent in the darkness that it was not for some seconds I thought of looking for the bolide, but even then I was in time to see it declining just before extinction. Others who have been out with their guns have, of course, seen exactly the same things ; I do not mention them to claim for myself any special powers of observation, but as instances of the way in which sport brings one in contact with nature. Other sportsmen, too, must have smiled at the marvel made of such appearances by clever and well-educated, but indoor, people.

This very spring (1883), as I walked about a town in the evening, I used to listen to find if I could hear any one mention the zodiacal light, which, just after sunset, was distinctly visible for a fortnight at a time. It was more than usually distinct, a perfect cone, reaching far up into the sky among the western stars. No one seemed to observe it, though it faced them evening after evening. Here was an instance in the opposite direction—a curious phenomenon, even now rather the subject of hypothesis than of demonstration, entirely overlooked. The common phenomenon made a marvel, and the unexplained phenomenon unnoticed. Both in the eyes of a thoughtful person are equally wonderful ; but that point of view

is apart from my present object, which is to show that
sport trains the eye. As a boy, roving about the
hedges with my gun, it was my especial delight to see
Mercury, because one of the great astronomers had never
seen that planet, and because in all the books it was
stated as difficult to see. The planet was favourably
situated, and I used to see it constantly after sunset
then, pale, and but just outside the sunset glow, only
a little way above the distant hills. Now it is curious,
to remark in passing, that as the sun sets behind a hill
the slope of the hill towards you is often obscured by
his light. It appears a luminous misty surface, rosy-
tinted, and this luminous mist hides the trees upon
it, so that the slope is apparently nothing but a
broad sweep of colour; while those hills opposite the
sun, even if twice as distant, are so clearly defined that
the smallest object is evident upon them. Sometimes,
instead of the mist on the western hill, there is a blood-
like purple almost startling in its glory of light.

There have been few things I have read of, or
studied, which in some manner or other I have not
seen illustrated in this country while out in the fields.
It is said that in the Far West, on the level prairies,
when the snow covers them, you see miles and miles
away, a waggon stopping; you hurry on, and in half a
day's journey overtake it, to find the skull of an ox—
so greatly has distance and the mirage of the snow
magnified its apparent size. But a few days since I
saw some rooks on the telegraph wires against a bright
sky, but as I approached they flew and resolved into
starlings, so much had the brilliant light deceived me.
A hare sometimes, on the open ground, looks at a

distance, in the sunny days of May when hares are often abroad in daylight, as big as a good-sized dog, and, except by the leap and the absence of visible tail, can hardly be told from a dog. The bamboo fishing-rods, if you will glance at the bamboo itself as you fish, seem the most singular of growths. There is no wood in the hedge like it, neither ash, hazel, oak, sapling, nor anything ; it is thoroughly foreign, almost unnatural. The hard knots, the hollow stem, the surface glazed so as to resist a cut with a knife and nearly turn the steel—this is a tropical production alone. But while working round the shore presently you come to the sedges, and by the sedges stands a bunch of reeds. A reed is a miniature bamboo, the same shape, the same knots, and glazy surface ; and on reference to any intelligent work of botany, it appears that they both belong to the same order of inward-growing Endogens, so that a few moments bestowed on the reed by the waters give a clear idea of the tropical bamboo, and make the singular foreign production home-like and natural.

I found, while I was shooting every day, that the reeds, and ferns, and various growths through which I pushed my way, explained to me the jungles of India, the swamps of Central Africa, and the back-woods of America ; all the vegetation of the world. Representatives exist in our own woods, hedges, and fields, or by the shore of inland waters. It was the same with flowers. I think I am scientifically accurate in saying that every known plant has a relative of the same species or genus, growing wild in this country. The very daisy, the commonest of all, contains a volume of botany ; so do the heaths, and the harebells

that hang so heavily under the weight of the September
dew.   The horse-tails by the shore carry the imagination further back into the prehistoric world when re-
lations of these plants flourished as trees.   The horse-
tails by ponds are generally short, about a foot or
eighteen inches high, more or less, but in ditches occasionally there are specimens of the giant horse-tail as
high as the waistcoat, with a stem as thick as a walking-
stick.   This is a sapling from which the prehistoric tree
can readily be imagined.   From our southern woods the
wild cat has been banished, but still lives in the north
as an English representative of that ferocious feline
genus which roams in tropical forests.   We still have
the deer, both wild and in parks.   Then there are the
birds, and these, in the same manner as plants, represent the inhabitants of the trackless wilds abroad.
Happily the illustration fails mostly in reptiles, which
need not be regretted; but even these, in their general
outline as it were, are presented.

It has long been one of my fancies that this country
is an epitome of the natural world, and that if any one
has come really into contact with its productions, and is
familiar with them, and what they mean and represent,
then he has a knowledge of all that exists on the earth.
It holds good even of Australia; for palæontologists
produce fossil remains of marsupials or kangaroos.   As
for the polar conditions, when going round for snipes I
constantly saw these in miniature.   The planing action
of ice was shown in the ditches, where bridges of ice
had been formed; these slipping, with a partial thaw,
smoothed the grasses and mars of teazles in the higher
part of the slope, and then lower down, as the pressure

increased, cut away the earth, exposing the roots of grasses, and sometimes the stores of acorns laid up by mice. Frozen again in the night, the glacier stayed, and crumbling earth, leaves, fibres, acorns, and small dead boughs fell on it. Slipping on as the wind grew warmer, it carried these with it and deposited them fifty yards from where they originated. This is exactly the action of a glacier. The ice-mist was often visible over the frozen water-meadows, where I went for duck, teal, and at intervals a woodcock in the adjacent mounds. But it was better seen in the early evening over a great pond, a mile or more long; where, too, the immense lifting power of water, was exemplified, as the merest trickle of a streamlet flowing in by-and-by forced up the thick ice in broad sheets weighing hundreds of tons. Then, too, breathing-holes formed just as they are described in the immense lakes of North America, Lakes Superior or Michigan, and in the ice of the Polar circle. These were never frozen over and attracted wild-fowl.

In August, when there were a few young ducks about, the pond used to remind me in places of the tropical lakes we heard so much of after the explorers got through the portentous continent, on account of the growth of aquatic weeds, the quantity and extent of which no one would credit who had not seen them. No wonder the explorers could not get through the papyrus-grown rivers and lakes, for a boat could hardly be forced through these. Acres upon acres of weeds covered the place, some coming up from a depth of twelve feet. Some fish are chiefly on the feed in the morning, and any one who has the courage

to get up at five will find them ravenous. We often
visited the place a little after that hour. A swim was
generally the first thing, and I mention a swim because
it brings me to the way in which this mere pond
illustrated the great ocean which encircles the world.
For it is well known that the mighty ocean is belted
with currents, the cold water of the Polar seas seeking
the warmth of the Equator, and the warm water of the
Equator floating—like the Gulf Stream—towards the
Pole, floating because (I think I am right) the warm
water runs on the surface. The favourite spot for
swimming in our pond was in such a position that a
copse cast a wide piece of water there into deep shadow
all the morning up till ten o'clock at least. At six in the
morning this did not matter, all the water was of much
the same temperature; having been exposed to the
night everywhere, it was cold of course.

But after ten the thing was different; by that time
the hot reaper's sun had warmed the surface of the open
water on which the rays fell almost from the moment
the sun rose.   Towards eleven o'clock the difference in
temperature was marked ; but those who then came to
bathe, walking along the shore or rowing, dipped their
hands in and found the water warm, and anticipated
that it would be equally so at the bathing-place. So
it was at the surface, for the warm water had begun
to flow in, and the cold water out, rather deeper, setting
up, in fact, an exact copy of the current of the ocean,
the shadowed part by the copse representing the Polar
area.   Directly any one began to swim he found the
difference, the legs went down into cold water, and in
many cases cramp ensued with alarming results and

danger. Down to the chest it was warm, quite warm, while the feet were very cold. Not much imagination is needed to conceive the effect on persons not used to rough bathing, and even a strong man might suffer. People insisted that these chills and cramps were caused by cold springs rising at the bottom, and could not be argued out of that belief. As a matter of fact there was not a single spring over the whole extent of the bottom. That part in particular was often dry, not from dry weather, but as the water of the pond was drawn away. Let it rain as much as it would, no spring ever broke up there. The cold currents were produced by the shadow of the copse, and, had the trees been felled, would have disappeared. That would have been like letting the sun of the Equator shine on the Polar seas.

After a storm of wind the lee shore was marked with a dark-green line of weeds and horse-tails, torn up and drifted across, which had been thrown up by the little breakers beyond the usual level of the water. A mass of other weeds and horse-tails, boughs and leaves, remained floating; and now was seen a reversal of the habits of fishes. Every one knows that fishes seek the windward shore in a breeze for the insects blown in; but now, while the gale, though subsiding, still rippled the water, the best place to fish was on the lee shore, just at the edge of the drifted weeds. Various insects probably were there washed away from the green raft to which they had clung. The water being often lowered by drawing hatches, the level changed frequently; and ·as storms of wind happened at different levels, so there were several little raised beaches showing where the level had been, formed of washed gravel and stones—the counterpart, in fact, of the raised beaches of the geologists. When the water was almost all drawn off, then there was a deep winding channel in the mud of the bottom, along which trickled a little streamlet which fed the pond. The sun hardening the mud, it was possible by-and-by to walk to the edge of the channel, where it could be seen that the streamlet ran five or six feet deep between precipitous banks of mud.

Near where the stream first entered the pond the deposit was much deeper, for this five feet of alluvium had, in fact, been brought down by one small brook in the course of little more than fifty years. The pond had been formed fifty years previously, but already in so short a period, geologically speaking, all that end was silting up, and the little brook was making a delta, and a new land was rising from the depths of the wave. This is exactly what has happened on an immensely larger scale in the history of the earth, and any one who had seen it, and knew the circumstances, could comprehend the enormous effects produced in geological time by rivers like the Ganges, the Amazon, or Nile. Going by with a gun so frequently, one could not help noticing these things, and remembering them when reading Lyell's "Geology," or Maury's book on the sea, or the innumerable treatises bearing on the same interesting questions. Whether *en route* for the rabbit-ground, or looking for water-fowl, or later for snipe, I never passed by without finding something, often a fragment of fossil washed from the gravel or sand by the last storm.

NATURE AND THE GAMEKEEPER.

THE changes in the fauna of the inland counties brought about by the favour shown to certain species are very remarkable. The alterations caused by the preservation of pheasants have reached their limit. No further effects are likely to be produced, even if pheasant-preserving should be carried to a still greater extent, which itself is improbable. One creature at least, the pine-marten, has been exterminated over Southern England, and is now only to be seen—in the stuffed state—in museums. It may be roughly described as a large tree-weasel, and was shot down on account of its habit of seizing pheasants at roost. The polecat is also practically extinct, though occasional specimens are said to occur. These two animals could not be allowed to exist in any preserve. But it is in the list of birds that the change is most striking. Eagles are gone: if one is seen it is a stray from Scotland or Wales; and so are the buzzards, except from the moors. Falcons are equally rare: the little merlin comes down from the north now and then, but the peregrine falcon as a resident or regular visitor is extinct. The hen-harrier is still shot at intervals; but the large hawks have ceased out of the daily life, as it were, of woods and fields. Horned owls are becoming rare ; even the barn-owl has all but disappeared from some districts, and the wood-owl is local. The raven is extinct— quite put out. The birds are said to exist near the sea-coast; but it is certain that any one may walk over inland country for years without seeing one. These, being all more or less birds of prey, could not but be excluded from pheasant-covers. All these birds, however, would probably resume their ancient habitations in the course of five-and-twenty years if permitted to do so. They exist plentifully at no great distance—judged as such strong flyers judge distance ; and if they found that they were unmolested they would soon come back from the extremities of the land.

But even more remarkable than the list of birds driven away is the list of those creatures, birds and animals, which have stood their ground in spite of traps, guns, and dogs. Stoats and weasels are always shot when seen, they are frequently trapped, and in every manner hunted to the death and their litters destroyed—the last the most effectual method of extermination. But in spite of the unceasing enmity directed against them, stoat and weasel remain common. They still take their share of game, both winged and ground. Stoat and weasel will not be killed out. As they are both defenceless creatures, and not even swift of foot, being easily overtaken in the open, their persistent continuance is curious. If any reason can be assigned for it, it must be because they spend much of their time in buries, where they are comparatively safe, and because they do not confine themselves to

woods, but roam cornfields and meadows. Certainly,
if man has tried to exterminate any creature, he has
tried his hardest to get rid of these two, and has failed.
It is even questionable whether their numbers show
any appreciable diminution. Kept down to the utmost
in one place, they flourish in another. Kestrel and
sparrowhawk form a parallel among winged creatures.
These two hawks have been shot, trapped, and their
eggs destroyed unsparingly: they remain numerous
just the same. Neither of them choose inaccessible
places for their eyries; neither of them rear large
broods. The sparrowhawk makes a nest in a tree,
often in firs; the kestrel lays in old rooks', crows', or
magpies' nests. Both the parents are often shot on or
near the nest, and the eggs broken. Sometimes the
young are permitted to grow large enough to fly, and
are then shot down after the manner of rook-shooting.
Nevertheless kestrels are common, and sparrowhawks,
if not quite so numerous, are in no degree uncommon.
Perhaps the places of those killed are supplied by
birds from the great woods, moors, and mountains of
the north.

A third instance is the crow. Hated by all game-
keepers and sportsmen, by farmers, and every one who
has anything to do with country life, the crow sur-
vives. Cruel tyrant as he is to every creature smaller
than himself, not a voice is raised in his favour.
Yet crows exist in considerable numbers. Shot off in
some places, they are recruited again from others where
there is less game preservation. The case of the crow,
however, is less striking than that of the two hawks;
because the crow is a cosmopolitan bird, and if every

o

specimen in the British Isles were destroyed to-day
there would be an influx from abroad in a very short
time. The crow is, too, partly a sea-coast feeder, and
so escapes. Still, to any one who knows how determined is the hostility to his race shown by all country-
people, his existence in any number must be considered
remarkable. His more powerful congener the raven,
as has been pointed out, is practically extinct in
southern counties, and no longer attacks the shepherd's
weakly lambs. Why, then, does the crow live on ?
Wherever a pair of ravens do exist the landowner
generally preserves them now, as interesting representatives of old times. They are taken care of ; people
go to see them ; the appearance of eggs in the nest is
recorded. But the raven does not multiply. Barn
owls live on, though not in all districts. Influenced
by the remonstrance of naturalists, many gentlemen
have stopped the destruction of owls ; but a custom
once established is not easily put an end to.

Jays and magpies have also been subjected to a bitter
warfare of extermination. Magpies are quite shot off
some places; in others they exist sparingly ; here and
there they may be found in fair numbers. Occasionally their nests are preserved—indeed, the growing
tendency is to spare. Still, they have been shot off
rigorously, and have survived it. So have jays. In
large woods—particularly where there is much fir—
jays are so numerous that to destroy them seems
almost impossible. Another bird that has defied the
gun and trap is the green woodpecker, which used to
be killed for alleged destruction of timber. Woodpeckers are not now so ceaselessly killed, though the

old system of slaying them is common enough. They have defied not only gun and trap, but the cunning noose placed at the mouth of their holes.

Twenty creatures, furred and feathered, have undergone severe persecution since the extension of pheasant covers, and of these the first nine have more or less succumbed—namely, pine-marten, polecat, eagle, buzzard, falcon, kite, horned owl, harrier, and raven. The remaining eleven have survived—namely, stoat, weasel, rat, crow, kestrel, sparrowhawk, brown and barn owl, jay, magpie, and woodpecker. Pheasants of themselves are not responsible for all this warfare and all these changes; but the pheasant-cover means more than pheasants, or rather has done. Rabbits required even more protection from furred enemies; the head of rabbits kept up in many places practically paid the keeper's wages. This warfare in its fiercest form may be roughly said to be coeval with the invention of the percussion gun, and to have raged now for over half a century. The resistance, therefore, of the various species has been fairly tested, and we may reasonably conclude that no further disappearance will take place, unless by the destruction of woods themselves. One new bird only has been introduced into England since the pheasant—the red-legged partridge—which seems to be fairly established in some districts, not to the entire satisfaction of sportsmen. One new bird has also been introduced into Scotland—in this case a re-introduction. The magnificent capercailzie is now flourishing again in the north, to the honour of those who laboured for its restoration. In these notes I have not included attempts at acclimatization, as that of the wild turkey from North America, which has partly succeeded. Beavers, too, have been induced to resume possession of their ancient streams under careful supervision, but they are outside present consideration. While England has thus lost some species and suffered a diminution of several, other countries have been supplied from our streams and woods and hedge-rows. England has sent the sparrow to the United States and Australia; also the nightingale, rabbit, salmon, trout, and sweet-briar.

It is quite open to argument that pheasant-covers have saved as well as destroyed. Wood-pigeons could scarcely exist in such numbers without the quiet of preserved woods to breed in ; nor could squirrels. Nor can the rarity of such birds as the little bearded tit be charged on game. The great bustard, the crane, and bittern have been driven away by cultivation. The crane, possibly, has deserted us wilfully ; since civilization in other countries has not destroyed it. And then the fashion of making natural history collections has much extended of recent years : so much so that many blame too ardent collectors for the increasing rarity of birds like the crossbill, waxwing, hoopoe, golden oriole, and others which seem to have once visited this country more commonly than at present.

THE SACRIFICE TO TROUT.

How much the breeding of pheasants has told upon the existence of other creatures in fur and feathers I have already shown; and much the same thing is true of the preservation of trout. There is this difference, however: that while the pheasant has now produced its utmost effect, the alterations due to trout are increasing. Trout are now so highly and so widely preserved that the effect cannot but be felt. Their preservation in the numbers now considered necessary entails the destruction of some and the banishment of other creatures. The most important of these is the otter. Guns, dogs, traps set under water so as not to be scented; all modes of attack are pressed into the service, and it is not often that he escapes. When traces of an otter were found, a little while since, in the Kennet—he had left his mark on the back of a trout—the fact was recorded with as much anxiety as if a veritable wolf had appeared. With such animosity has the otter been hunted that he is becoming one of the rarest of wild animals here in the south. He is practically extinct on the majority of southern streams, and has been almost beaten off the Thames itself. But the otter is not likely to be exterminated in the sense that the wolf has been. Otters will be found elsewhere in England long after the last of them has disappeared from the south. Next the pike must be ousted from trout-streams. Special nets have been invented by which pike can be routed from their strongholds. Much hunting about quickens the intelligence of the pike to such a degree that he cannot be secured in the ordinary manner; he baffles the net by keeping close to the bank, behind stones, or by retiring to holes under roots. Perch have to go as well as pike; and then comes the turn of birds.

Herons, kingfishers, moorhens, coots, grebes, ducks, teal, various divers, are all proscribed on behalf of trout. Herons are regarded as most injurious to a fishery. As was observed a century ago, a single heron will soon empty a pond or a stretch of brook. As their long necks give them easy command of a wide radius in spying round them, it is rather difficult to shoot them with a shot-gun; but with the small-bore rifles now made no heron is safe. They are generally shot early in the morning. Were it not for the fact that herons nest like rooks, and that heronries are valued appurtenances in parks, they would soon become scarce. Kingfishers prey on smaller fish, but are believed to eat almost as many as herons. Kingfishers resort in numbers to trout nurseries, which are as traps for them : and there they are more than decimated. Owls are known to take fish occasionally, and are therefore shot. The greatest loss sustained in fisheries takes place in the spawning season, and again when the fry are about. Some students of fish-life believe that almost all wild-fowl will swallow the ova and fry of trout. It must be understood that I am not here entering into the question whether all these are really so injurious; I am merely giving a list of the "dogs with a bad name." Moorhens and coots are especially disliked because they are on or near the water day and night, and can clear off large quantities of fry. Grebes (di-dappers or dabchicks) are similar in habit, but less destructive because fewer. Ducks are ravenous devourers; teal are equally hated. The various divers which occasionally visit the streams are also guilty. Lastly, the swan is a well-known trout-pirate. Besides these, the two kinds of rat—land and water—have a black mark against them. Otter, pike, perch, heron, kingfisher, owl, moorhen, coot, grebe, diver, wild-duck, swan, teal, dipper, land-rat, and water-rat—altogether sixteen creatures—are killed in order that one may flourish. Although none of these, even in the south of England— except the otter—has yet been excluded, the majority of them are so thinned down as to be rarely seen unless carefully sought.

To go through the list: otters are practically excluded; the pike is banished from trout streams but is plentiful in others; so too with perch; herons, much reduced in numbers; owls, reduced; kingfishers, growing scarce; coots, much less numerous because not permitted to nest; grebes, reduced; wild-duck, seldom seen in summer, because not permitted to nest; teal, same; swan, not permitted on fisheries unless ancient rights protect it; divers, never numerous, now scarcer; moorhens, still fairly plentiful because their ranks are constantly supplied from moats and ponds where they

breed under semi-domestic conditions. The draining
of marsh-lands and levels began the exile of wild-fowl;
and now the increasing preservation of trout adds to
the difficulties under which these birds strive to retain
a hold upon inland waters. The Thames is too long
and wide for complete exclusion; but it is surprising
how few moorhens even are to be seen along the river.
Lesser rivers are still more empty, as it were, of life.
The great osier-beds still give shelter to some, but not
nearly so many as formerly. Up towards the spring-
heads, where the feeders are mere runlets, the scarcity
of wild-fowl has long been noticed. Hardly a wild-
duck is now seen; one or two moorhens or a dabchick
seem all. Coots have quite disappeared in some
places: they are shot on ponds, having an ill reputation for the destruction of the fry of coarse or pond
fish, as well as of trout. Not all these changes, indeed,
are attributable to trout alone; but the trout holds
a sort of official position and leads the van. Our
southern rivers, with the exception of the Thames, are
for the most part easily preserved.

They run through cultivated country, with meadows
or cornfields, woods or copses, and rarely far through
open, unenclosed land. A stranger, and without per-
mission, would often find it difficult to walk half a
mile along the bank of such a stream as this. Consequently, if it is desired to preserve it, the riparian
owners can do so to the utmost, and the water-fowl
considered injurious to fish can as easily be kept down.
It is different in the north, for instance, where the
streams have a background of moors, mountains, tarns,
and lakes. In these their fastnesses birds find some

security. From the coast they are also recruited;
while on our southern coasts it is a source of lament
that wild-fowl are not nearly so plentiful as formerly.
Of course in winter it often happens that a flock of
wild-fowl alight in passing; but how long do they stay?
The real question is, how many breed? Where trout
are carefully preserved, very few indeed; so that it is
evident trout are making as much difference as the
pheasants. Trout preservation has become much more
extended since the fish has been studied and found
to be easily bred. Advertisements are even put forward recommending people to keep trout instead of
poultry, since they can be managed with certainty. It
seems reasonable, therefore, to suppose that the influence of trout on wild creatures will continue to
extend for some time yet. Already where trout preservation has been carefully carried out it has produced a visible impression upon their ranks. In ten
years, if it were abandoned, most of these creatures
would be plentiful again on the waters from which
they have been driven; I should myself be very glad
to see many of them back again.

But if preservation has excluded many creatures, it
has also saved many. Badgers, in all probability, would
be extinct—really extinct, like the wolf—were it not
for the seclusion of covers. Without the protection
which hunting affords them, foxes would certainly
have disappeared. The stag and fallow-deer are other
examples; so, too, the wild white cattle maintained
in a few parks. In a measure the rook owes its
existence to protection; for although naturalists have
pointed out its usefulness, the rook is no favourite

with agriculturists. Woodcocks, again, are protected, and are said to have increased, though it is open to question if their increased numbers may not be due to other causes. Cultivation banishes wild geese and snipe, but adds to the numbers of small birds, I fancy, and very probably to the number of mice. When the country was three-fourths champaign—open, unenclosed, and uncultivated—it cannot be supposed that so many grain-eating birds found sustenance as now. The subject is capable of much development. Enough, however, has been said to show that Nature at present is under artificial restraints; but her excluded creatures are for the most part ready to return if ever those restraints are removed.

THE HOVERING OF THE KESTREL.

THERE has lately been some discussion about the hovering of kestrels: the point being whether the bird can or cannot support itself in the air while stationary, without the assistance of one or more currents of air. The kestrel is the commonest hawk in the southern parts of England, so that many opportunities occur to observe his habits; and there ought not to be any doubt in the matter. It is even alleged that it will go far to decide the question of the possibility of flight or of the construction of an aerial machine. Without entering into this portion of the discussion, let us examine the kestrel's habits.

This hawk has a light easy flight, usually maintaining an altitude a little lower than the tallest elms, but higher than most trees. He will keep this particular altitude for hours together, and sweep over miles of country, with only occasional variations—excluding, of course, descents for the purpose of taking mice. It is usually at this height that a kestrel hovers, though he is capable of doing it at a much greater elevation. As he comes gliding through the atmosphere, suddenly he shoots up a little (say, roughly, two or three feet), and then stops short. His tail, which is broader than it looks, is bent slightly downwards ; his wings beat the air, at the first glance, just as if he was progressing. Sometimes he seems to oscillate to one side, sometimes to the other; but these side movements do not amount to any appreciable change of position. If there be little or no wind (note this) he remains beating the air, to the eye at least perfectly stationary, perhaps as much as half a minute or more. He then seems to slip forward about half a yard, as if a pent-up force was released, but immediately recovers himself and hovers again. This alternate hovering and slipping forward may be repeated two or three times : it seems to depend on the bird's judgment as to the chance of prey. If he does not think a mouse is to be had, at the first slip he allows himself to proceed. If the spot be likely, or (what is still more tempting) if it is near a place where he has taken prey previously, he will slip and bring up several times. Now and then he will even fetch a half-circle when his balance or impetus (or both) is quite exhausted, and so return to the same spot and recommence. But this is not often, as a rule, after two or three slips he proceeds on his voyage. He will repeat the same round day after day, if undisturbed, and, if the place be at all infested with mice, he will come to it three or four times a day. There is, therefore, every chance of watching him, if you have once found his route. Should he spy a mouse, down he comes, quick but steady, and very nearly straight upon it. But kestrels do not always descend upon prey actually in view. Unless I am much mistaken, they now and then descend in a likely

spot and watch like a cat for a minute or two for mice
or beetles. For rest they always seek a tree.

Now, having briefly sketched his general manner,
et us return and examine the details. In the first
place, he usually rises slightly, with outstretched
wings, as if about to soar at the moment of com-
mencing hovering. The planes of the wings are then
inclined, and meet the air. At the instant of stopping, the tail is depressed. It appears reasonable to
conjecture that the slight soaring is to assist the tail
in checking his onward course, and to gain a balance.
Immediately the wings beat rapidly, somewhat as they
do in ordinary flight but with a more forward motion,
and somewhat as birds do when about to perch on
an awkward ledge, as a swallow at an incomplete
nest under an eave. The wings look more, in front, as
if attached to his neck. In an exaggerated way ducks
beat the air like this, with no intention of rising at
all, merely to stretch their wings. The duck raises
himself as he stands on the ground, stretches himself
to his full height, and flaps his wings horizontally.
The kestrel's wings strike downwards and a very
little forwards, for his natural tendency is to slip
forwards, and the object of slightly reversing his
vanes is to prevent this and yet at the same time to
support him. His shape is such that if he were rigid
with outstretched wings he would glide ahead, just as
a ship in a calm slowly forges ahead because of her
lines, which are drawn for forward motion. The
kestrel's object is to prevent his slip forwards, and the
tail alone will not do it. It is necessary for him to
" stroke " the air in order to keep up at all ; because

the moment he pauses gravitation exercises a force much greater that when he glides.

While hovering there are several forces balanced: first, the original impetus onwards; secondly, that of the depressed tail dragging and stopping that onward course; thirdly, that of the wing beating downwards; and fourthly, that of the wing a very little reversed beating forwards, like backing water with a scull. When used in the ordinary way the shape of the wing causes it to exert a downward and a backward pressure. His slip is when he loses balance: it is most obviously a loss of balance; he quite oscillates sometimes when it occurs; and now and then I have seen a kestrel unable to catch himself, and obliged to proceed some distance before he could hover again. Occasionally, in the slip he loses a foot or so of elevation, but not always. While actually hovering, his altitude does not vary an inch. All and each of these movements and the considerations to which they give rise show conclusively that the act of hovering is nothing more or less than an act of balancing; and when he has his balance he will rest a moment with outstretched wings kept still. He uses his wings with just sufficient force neither to rise nor fall, and prevents progress by a slightly different stroke.

The next point is, Where does he hover? He hovers any and everywhere, without the slightest choice. He hovers over meadows, cornfields; over the tops of the highest downs, sometimes at the very edge of a precipice or above a chalk quarry; over gardens, waste ground; over the highway; over summer and other ricks and thatched sheds, from which he sometimes takes his prey; over stables, where mice abound. He has no preference for one side of a hedge or grove, and cares not the least on which the wind blows. His hovering is entirely determined by his judgment as to the chance of prey. I have seen a kestrel hover over every variety of dry ground that is to be found.

Next, as to the wind. If any one has read what has preceded upon his manner of preserving his balance, it must be at once apparent that, supposing a kestrel were hovering in a calm and a wind arose, he would at once face it, else his balance could not be kept. Even on the ground almost all birds face the wind by choice; but the hovering kestrel has no choice. He must hover facing the wind, or it would upset him: just as you may often see a rook flung half aback by a sudden gust. Hence has arisen the supposition that a kestrel cannot hover without a wind. The truth is, he can hover in a perfect calm, and no doubt could do so in a room if it were large enough. He requires no current of any kind, neither a horizontal breeze nor an ascending current. A kestrel can and does hover in the dead calm of summer days, when there is not the faintest breath of wind. He will and does hover in the still, soft atmosphere of early autumn, when the gossame falls in showers, coming straight down as if it were raining silk. If you puff up a ball of thistledown it will languish on your breath and sink again to the sward. The reapers are sweltering in the wheat, the keeper suffocates in the wood, the carter walks in the

shadow cast by his load of corn, the country-side stare,
all parched and cracked and gasps for a rainy breeze.
The kestrel hovers just the same. Could he not do
so, a long calm would half starve him, as that is his
manner of preying. Having often spent hours in trees
for the purpose of a better watch upon animals and
birds, I can vouch for it that ascending currents are
not frequent—rare, in fact, except in a gale. In a
light air or calm there is no ascending current, or it
is imperceptible and of no use to the kestrel. Such
currents, when they do exist, are very local; but the
kestrel's hover is not local: he can hover anywhere.
He can do it in the face of a stiff gale, and in a perfect
calm. The only weather he dislikes is heavy thunder,
rain, or hail, during which he generally perches on a
tree; but he can hover in all ordinary rain. He effects
it by sheer power and dexterity of wing. Therefore if
the fact has any bearing upon the problem of flight,
the question of currents may be left out altogether.
His facing the wind is, as has been pointed out, only a
proof that he is keeping his balance.

The kestrel is not the only bird that hovers. The
sparrowhawk can. So can all the finches, more or
less, when taking seeds from a plant which will not
bear their weight or which they cannot otherwise get
at; also when taking insects on the wing. Sparrows
do the same. Larks hover in their mating season,
uttering a short song, not the same as when they soar.
Numerous insects can hover: the great dragon-fly will
stop dead short in his rapid flight, and stay suspended
till it suits him to advance. None of these require
any current or wind. I do not think that hovering

requires so much strength of wing or such an exercise of force as when birds rise almost straight up. Snipes do it, and woodcocks ; so also pheasants, rocketing with tremendous effort; so also a sparrow in a confined court, rising almost straight to the slates. Evidently this needs great power. Hovering is very interesting ; but not nearly so mysterious as at least one other power possessed by birds.

P

BIRDS CLIMBING THE AIR.

Two hawks come over the trees, and, approaching each other, rise higher into the air. They wheel about for a little without any apparent design, still rising, when one ceases to beat the air with his wings, stretches them to their full length, and seems to lean aside. His impetus carries him forward and upward, at the same time in a circle, something like a skater on one foot. Revolving round a centre, he rises in a spiral, perhaps a hundred yards across; screwing upwards, and at each turn ascending half the diameter of the spiral. When he begins this it appears perfectly natural, and nothing more than would necessarily result if the wings were held outstretched and one edge of the plane slightly elevated. The impulse of previous flight, the beat of strong pinions, and the swing and rush of the bird evidently suffice for two or three, possibly for four or five, winding movements, after which the retarding effects of friction and gravitation ought, according to theory, to gradually bring the bird to a stop. But up goes the hawk, round and round like a woodpecker climbing a tree; only the hawk has nothing tangible into which to stick his claws and to rest his tail against. Those winding circles must surely cease; his own weight alone must stop him, and those wide wings outstretched must check his course. Instead of which the hawk rises as easily as at first, and without the slightest effort— no beat of wing or flutter, without even a slip or jerk, easily round and round. His companion does the same; often, perhaps always, revolving the opposite way, so as to face the first. It is a fascinating motion to watch.

The graceful sweeping curl holds the eye : it is a line of beauty, and draws the glance up into the heights of the air. The darker upper part of one is usually visible at the same time as the lighter under part of the other, and as the dark wheels again the sunlight gleams on the breast and under wing. Sometimes they take regular curves, ascending in an equal degree with each ; each curve representing an equal height gained perpendicularly. Sometimes they sweep round in wide circles, scarcely ascending at all. Again, suddenly one will shoot up almost perpendicularly, immediately followed by the other. Then they will resume the regular ascent. Up, like the woodpecker round a tree, till now the level of the rainy scud which hurries over in wet weather has long been past; up till to the eye it looks as if they must soon attain to the flecks of white cloud in the sunny sky to-day. They are in reality far from that elevation; but their true height is none the less wonderful. Resting on the sward, I have watched them go up like this through a lovely morning atmosphere till they seemed about to actually enter the blue, till they were smaller in appearance than larks at their highest ascent, till the head had to be thrown right back to see them. This last circumstance shows how perpendicularly they ascend, winding round a line drawn straight up. At their very highest they are hardly visible, except when the under wing and breast passes and gleams in the light.

All this is accomplished with outstretched wings held at full length, without flap, or beat, or any apparent renewal of the original impetus. If you take a flat stone and throw it so that it will spin, it will go some way straight, then rise, turn aside, describe a half-circle, and fall. If the impetus kept in it, it would soar like the hawk, but this does not happen. A boomerang acts much in the same manner, only more perfectly: yet, however forcibly thrown, the impetus soon dies out of a boomerang. A skater gets up his utmost speed, suddenly stands on one foot, and describes several circles; but in two minutes comes to a standstill, unless he "screws," or works his skate, and so renews the impulse. Even at his best he only goes round, and does not raise his weight an inch from the ice. The velocity of a bullet rapidly decreases, and a ball shot from an express rifle, and driven by a heavy charge, soon begins to droop. When these facts are duly considered, it will soon be apparent what a remarkable feat soaring really is. The hawk does not always ascend in a spiral, but every now and then revolves in a circle—a flat circle—and suddenly shoots up with renewed rapidity. Whether this be merely sportive wantonness or whether it is a necessity, is impossible to determine; but to me it does not appear as if the hawk did it from necessity. It has more the appearance of variation : just as you or I might walk fast at one moment and slowly at another, now this side of the street and now the other. A shifting of the plane of the wings would, however, in all probability, give some impetus : the question is, would it be sufficient ? I have seen hawks go up in sunny and lovely weather—in fact, they seem to prefer still, calm weather; but, considering the height to which they attain, no one can positively assert that they do or do not utilize a current. If they do, they may be said to sail (a hawk's wings are technically his sails) round half the circle with the wind fair and behind, and then meet it the other half of the turn, using the impetus they have gained to surmount the breeze as they breast it. Granting this mechanical assistance, it still remains a wonderful feat, since the nicest adjustment must be necessary to get the impetus sufficient to carry the birds over the resistance. They do not drift, or very little.

My own impression is that a hawk can soar in a perfectly still atmosphere. If there is a wind he uses it; but it is quite as much an impediment as an aid. If there is no wind he goes up with the greater ease and to the greater height, and will of choice soar in a calm. The spectacle of a weight—for of course the hawk has an appreciable weight—apparently lifting itself in the face of gravitation and overcoming friction, is a very striking one. When an autumn leaf parts on a still day from the twig, it often rotates and travels some distance from the tree, falling reluctantly and

with pauses and delays in the air. It is conceivable
that if the leaf were animated and could guide its rotation, it might retard its fall for a considerable period
of time, or even rise higher than the tree.

COUNTRY LITERATURE.

I.—THE AWAKENING.

FOUR hundred years after the first printed book was sent out by Caxton the country has begun to read. An extraordinary reflection that twelve generations should pass away presenting the impenetrable front of indifference to the printing-press! The invention which travelled so swiftly from shore to shore till the remote cities of Mexico, then but lately discovered, welcomed it, for four centuries failed to enter the English counties. This incredible delay must not be supposed to be due to any exceptional circumstances or to inquisitorial action. The cause is found in the agricultural character itself. There has never been any difficulty in obtaining books in the country other than could be surmounted with patience. It is the peculiarity of knowledge that those who really thirst for it always get it. Books certainly came down in some way or other to Stratford-on-Avon, and the great mind that was growing there somehow found a means of reading them. Long, long before, when the printed page had not been dreamed of, the Grecian student, listening at the school, made his notes on oyster-shells and blade-bones. But here the will was wanting.

There was no prejudice, for no people admired learn
ing more than the village people, or gave it more
willing precedence. It was simple indifference, which
was mistaken for a lack of intelligence, but it was
most certainly nothing of the kind. How great, then,
must be the change when at last, after four hundred
years, the country begins to read!

To read everything and anything! The cottagers
in far-away hamlets, miles from a railway station, read
every scrap of printed paper that drifts across their
way, like leaves in autumn. The torn newspapers in
which the grocer at the market town wraps up their
weekly purchases, stained with tallow or treacle, are
not burned heedlessly. Some paragraph, some fragment of curious information, is gathered from the
pieces. The ploughman at his luncheon reads the
scrap of newspaper in which his bread-and-cheese was
packed for him. Men read the bits of paper in which
they carry their screws of tobacco. The stone-pickers
in spring in the meadows, often women, look at the bits
of paper scattered here and there before putting them
in their baskets. A line here and a line yonder, one
to-day, one to-morrow, in time make material equal
to a book. All information in our day filters through
the newspapers. There is no subject you can name of
which you may not get together a good body of
knowledge, often superior, because more recent, than
that contained in the best volumes, by watching the
papers and cutting out the paragraphs that relate to
it. No villager does that, but this ceaseless searching
for scraps comes to something like the same thing in
a more general manner.

London newspapers come now to the village and hamlet in all sorts of ways. Some by post, others by milk-cart, by carrier, by travellers; for country folk travel now, and invariably bring back papers bought at the railway book-stalls. After these have been read by the farmers and upper sort of people who purchased them, the fragments get out through innumerable channels to the cottages. The regular labourers employed on the farm often receive them as presents, and take nothing more gladly. If any one wishes to make a cottager a little present to show friendly remembrance, the best thing to send is a bundle of newspapers, especially, of course, if they are illustrated, which will be welcomed, and not a corner of the contents slurred over. Nothing is so contrary to fact as the common opinion that the agricultural labourer and his family are stupid and unintelligent. In truth, there are none who so appreciate information; and they are quite capable of understanding anything that may be sent them in print.

London papers of various descriptions come to the villages now in greatly increased numbers, probably fifteen or twenty for one that formerly arrived, and all these, or some portion of each, are nearly sure to be ultimately perused by some cottager. At the inns and beer-houses there is now usually a daily paper, unless the distance is farther than general to a station, and then there are weeklies with summaries of everything. So that the London press is accessible at the meanest beerhouse, and well bethumbed and besmeared the blackened sheets are, with holes where clumsy fingers have one through. The shepherd in his hut in the

lambing season, when the east wind blows and he
needs shelter, is sure to have a scrap of newspaper
with him to pore over in the hollow of the windy
downs. In summer he reads in the shade of the firs
while his sheep graze on the slope beneath. The
little country stations are often not stations at all
in the urban idea of such a convenience, being quite
distant from any town, and merely gathering together
the traffic from cross-roads. But the porters and men
who work there at times get a good many newspapers,
and these, after looking at them themselves, they take
or send up to their relatives in the village five or six
miles away. Everybody likes to tell another the
news; and now that there is such a village demand
for papers, to pass on a paper is like passing the news,
and gives a pleasure to donor and recipient.

So that papers which in days gone by would have
stopped where they first arrived now travel on and
circulate. If you had given a cottager a newspaper a
few years since he would have been silent and looked
glum. If you give him one now he says, "Thank you,"
briskly. He and his read anything and everything;
and as he walks beside the waggon he will pick up a
scrap of newspaper from the roadside and pore over it
as he goes. Girls in service send home papers from
London; so do the lads when from home—and so many
are away from home now. Papers come from Australia
and America; the latter are especial favourites on
account of the oddities with which the editors fill
the corners. No one ever talks of the Continent in
agricultural places; you hear nothing of France or
Germany; nothing of Paris or Vienna, which are not

so very distant in these days of railways, if distance
be measured by miles. London and London news is
familiar enough—they talk of London and of the
United States or Australia, but particularly of the
United States. The Continent does not exist to them;
but the United States is a sort of second home, and
he older men who have not gone sigh and say, "If I
had 'a emigrated, now you see, I should 'a done well."
There must be an immense increase in the number of
papers passing through country post-offices. That the
United States papers do come there is no doubt, for
they are generally taken up by the cottage people to
the farmhouses to show where the young fellows are
who have left the place. But the remarkable fact is
not in the increase of the papers, but in the growth of
the desire to read them—the demand of the country
for something to read.

In cottages of the better sort years ago you used to
find the most formal of old prints or coloured pictures
on the walls, stiff as buckram, unreal, badly executed,
and not always decent. The favourites now are
cuttings from the *Illustrated London News* or the
Graphic, with pictures from which many cottages in
the farthest away of the far country are hung round.
Now and then one may be entered which is perfectly
papered with such illustrations. These pictures in
themselves play no inconsiderable part in educating
the young, whose eyes become accustomed to correct
representations of scenes in distant places, and who
learn as much about such places and things as they
could do without personally going. Besides which,
the picture being found there is evidence that at

fourth or fifth, or it may be the tenth hand, the pape itself must have got there, and if it got there it was read.

The local press has certainly trebled in recent times, as may be learned by reference to any newspaper list and looking at the dates. The export, so to say, of type, machines, rollers, and the material of printing from London to little country places has equally grown. Now, these are not sent out for nothing, but are in effect paid for by the pennies collected in the crooked lanes and byways of rural districts. Besides the numerous new papers, there are the old-established ones whose circulation has enlarged. Altogether, the growth of the local country press is as remarkable in its way as was the expansion of the London press after the removal of the newspaper stamp. This is conclusive evidence of the desire to read, for a paper is a thing unsaleable unless some one wants to read it. They are for the most part weeklies, and their primary object is the collection of local information; but they one and all have excerpts rom London publications, often very well selected, and quite amusing if casually caught up by persons who may have fancied they knew something of London, current gossip, and the world at large. For you must go from home to learn the news; and if you go into a remote hamlet and take up the local paper you are extremely likely to light on some paragraph skilfully culled which will make an impression on you. It is with these excerpts that the present argument is chiefly concerned, the point being that they are important influences in the spread of general information. After the local gossip has been looked at the purchasers of these prints are sure to turn to these pieces, which serve them and theirs the most of the week to absorb.

II.—SCARCITY OF BOOKS.

Some little traffic in books, or rather pamphlets, goes on now in rural places through the medium of pedlars. There are not so many pedlars as was once the case, and those that remain are not men of such substance as their predecessors who travelled on foot with jewellery, laces, watches, and similar articles. The packmen who walk round the villages for tradesmen are a different class altogether: the pedlar does not confine himself to one district, and he sells for his own profit. In addition to the pins and ribbons, Birmingham jewellery, dream-books, and penny ballads, the pedlar now produces a bundle of small books, which are practically pamphlets, though in more convenient form than the ancient quartos. They are a miscellaneous lot, from fifty to one hundred and fifty pages; little monographs on one subject, tales, and especially such narratives as are drawn up and printed after a great calamity like the loss of the *Atalanta*. It is a curious fact that country people are much attracted to the sea, and the story of a shipwreck known to be true easily tempts the six-pences from their pockets. Dream-books and ballads sell as they always did sell, but for the rest the pedlar's bundle has nothing in it, as a rule, more pernicious than may be purchased at any little shop.

Romantic novelettes, reprints of popular and really clever stories, numbers of semi-religious essays and so on—some only stitched and without a wrapper— make up the show he spreads open before the cottage door or the servants at the farmhouse. Often the gipsy women, whose vans go slowly along the main roads while they make expeditions to the isolated houses in the fields, bring with them very similar bundles of publications. The sale of books has thus partly supplanted that of clothes-pegs and trumpery finery. Neither pedlars nor-gipsies would carry such articles as books unless there was a demand for them, and they thereby demonstrate the growth of the disposition to read.

There are no other persons engaged in circulating books in the actual country than these. In the windows of petty shops in villages it is common to see a local newspaper displayed as a sign that it is sold there; and once now and then, but not often, a few children's story-books, rather dingy, may be found. But the keepers of such shops are not awake to the new condition of things; very likely they cannot read themselves, and it does not occur to them that the people now growing up may have different feelings to those that were general in their own young days. In this inability to observe the change they are not alone. If it was explained to them, again, they would not know how to set about getting in a suitable stock; they would not know what to choose nor where to buy cheaply. Somebody would have to do it all for them. Practically, therefore, in the actual country there are no other traders distributing

cheap books than pedlars and gipsy women. Coming
in thence to those larger villages which possess a
market and are called towns—often only one long
street—there is generally a sort of curiosity shop,
kept perhaps by a cobbler, a carver and gilder, or
brazier, where odds and ends, as old guns and pistols,
renovated umbrellas, a stray portmanteau, rusty
fenders, and so forth, are for sale. Inside the window
are a few old books, with the brown and faded gilt
covers so common in days gone by, and on market
days these are put outside on the window-sill, or
perhaps a plank on trestles forming a bookstall. The
stray customers have hardly any connection with
the growing taste for reading, being people a little
outside the general run—gentlemen with archæological
or controversial tendencies, who never pass a dingy
cover without going as far as the title-page—visitors,
perhaps, at houses in the neighbourhood wandering
round to look at an ancient gateway or sun-dial left
from monastic days. Villagers beginning to read do
not care for this class of work; like children, they
look for something more amusing, and want something to wonder at for their money.

At the post-office there is often an assortment of
cheap stationery on sale, for where one cottager wrote
a letter a few years ago ten write them now. But
the shopkeeper—most likely a grocer or storekeeper
of some kind—knows nothing of books, and will tell
you, if you ask him, that he never sells any or has any
orders. How should he sell any, pray, when he does
not put the right sort into his window? He does not
think people read: he is occupied with moist sugar.

So that in these places literature is at a standstill. Proceeding onwards to the larger market town, which really is a town, perhaps a county town, or at least with a railway station, here one or two stationers may be found. One has a fair trade almost entirely with the middle-class people of the town; farmers when they drive in call for stationery, or for books if there is a circulating library, as there usually is. The villagers do not come to this shop; they feel that it is a little above them, and they are shy of asking for three pennyworth of writing-paper and envelopes. If they look in at the window in passing they see many well-bound books from 5s. to 10s., some of the more reputable novels, and educational manuals. The first they cannot afford; for the second they have not yet acquired the taste; the last repel them. This bookseller, though of course quite of a different stamp, and a man of business, would probably also declare that the villagers do not read. They do not come to him, and he is too busy to sit down and think about it. The other stationer's is a more humble establishment, where they sell cheap toys, Berlin wool, the weekly London papers with tales in them, and so on. The villagers who get as far as this more central town call here for their cheap stationery, their weekly London novelette, or tin trumpets for the children. But here, again, they do not order books, and rarely buy those displayed, for exactly the same reason as in the lesser village towns. The shopkeeper does not understand what they want, and they cannot tell him. They would know if they saw it; but till they see it they do not know themselves. There is no medium between the villager who wants to read and the books he would like. There is no machinery between the villager who wants to read and the London publisher. The villager is in utter ignorance of the books in the publisher's warehouse in London.

The villager who has just begun to read is in a position almost incomprehensible to a Londoner. The latter has seen books, books, books from boyhood always around him. He cannot walk down a street, enter an omnibus, go on a platform without having books thrust under his eyes. Advertisements a yard high glare at him from every hoarding, railway arch, and end-house facing a thoroughfare. In tunnels underground, on the very roofs above, book advertisements press upon his notice. It is impossible to avoid seeing them, even if he would. Books are everywhere—at home, at the reading-room, on the way to business; and on his return it is books, books, books. He buys a weekly paper, and book advertisements, book reviews, occupy a large part of it. Buy what sort of print he will—and he is always buying some sort from mere habit—books are pushed on him. If he is at all a student, or takes an interest—and what educated Londoner does not ?—in some political, scientific, or other question, he is constantly on the watch for publications bearing upon it. He subscribes to or sees a copy of one or other of the purely literary papers devoted to the examination of books, and has not the slightest difficulty in finding what he wants; the reviews tell him precisely the thing he requires to know, whether the volume will suit him or not. The reading Londoner is thus in constant contact with

Q

the publisher, as much as if the publisher spoke to
him across the breakfast table.

But the villager has never heard the publisher's
name; the villager never sees a literary review; he
has never heard, or, if so, so casually as not to
remember, the name of any literary paper describing
books.   When he gets hold of a London paper, the
parts which attract him are certainly not the advertisements; if he sees a book advertised there, it is by
chance.   Besides which, the advertisements in London
papers are, from necessity of cost, only useful to those
who frequently purchase books or have some reason
for keeping an eye on those that appear.   There are
thousands of books on publishers' shelves which have
been advertised, of course, but are not now ever put in
the papers.   So that when the villager gets a London
paper, as he does now much more frequently, the advertisements, if he sees them, are not designed for his
eye and do not attract him.   He never sees a gaudy
poster stuck on the side of the barn; there are no glazed
frames with advertisements in the sheds or hung on the
trees; the ricks are not covered, like the walls of
the London railway stations, with book advertisements, nor are they conspicuous on the waggons as
they are on the omnibuses.   When he walks down the
village there are no broad windows piled with books
higher than his head—books with the backs towards
him, books with the ornamented cover towards him,
books temptingly open at an illustration : nothing of
the sort.   There is not a book to be seen.   Some few
books are advertised in the local press and receive
notices—only a few, and these generally of a class too

expensive for him. Books of real value are usually
dear when first published. If he goes to a stationer's,
as already pointed out, for a few sheets of writing
paper and a packet of envelopes, he sees nothing displayed there to tempt him. Lastly, he hears no talking about books. Perhaps the most effective of all
advertisements in selling a book is conversation. If
people hear other people continually alluding to, or
quoting, or arguing about a book, they say, "We must
have it;" and they do have it. Conversation is the
very life of literature. Now, the villager never hears
anybody talk about a book.

III.—THE VILLAGER'S TASTE IN READING.

The villager could not even write down what he
would like to read, not yet having reached the stage
when the mind turns inwards to analyse itself. If
you unexpectedly put a boy with a taste for reading
in a large library and leave him to himself, he is at
a loss which way to turn or what to take from the
shelves. He proceeds by experiment looking at cover
after cover, half pulling out one, turning over a few
leaves of another, peeping into this, and so on, till
something seizes his imagination, when he will sit
down on the steps at once instead of walking across
the room to the luxurious easy-chair. The world of
books is to the villager far more unknown than to the
boy in the library, who has the books before him,
while the villager looks into vacancy. What the
villager would like can only be gathered from a variety

of little indications which hint at the unconsciou wishes of his mind.

First, the idea that he would require something easy and simple like a horn-book or primer must be dismissed. Villagers are not so simple by any means. Nor do they need something written in the plainest language, specially chosen, as words of one syllable are for children. What is designed for the village must not be written down to it. The village will reject rice and corn-flour—it will only accept strong meat. The subject must be strong, the manner strong, and the language powerful. Like the highest and most cultured minds—for extremes meet—the intelligence of the villagers naturally approves the best literature. Those authors whose works have a world-wide reputation (though totally unknown by name in hamlets sixty miles from London) would be the most popular. Their antiquity matters nothing; they would be new in the hamlet. When a gentleman furnishes a library he chooses representative authors—what are called library-books—first, forming a solid groundwork to the collection. These are the very volumes the country would like.

Every one when first exploring the world of books, and through them the larger world of reality, is attracted by travels and voyages. These are peculiarly interesting to country people, to whom the idea of exploration is natural. Reading such a book is like coming to a hill and seeing a fresh landscape spread out before them. There are no museums in the villages to familiarize them with the details of life in distant parts of the earth, so that every page as it is turned

over brings something new. They understand the
hardships of existence, hard food, exposure, the struggle
with the storm, and can enter into the anxieties and
privations of the earlier voyagers searching out the
coast of America. They would rather read these than
the most exciting novels. If they could get geography,
without degrees of longitude, geography, or rather
ethnography, which deals with the ways of the inhabitants, they would be delighted. All such facts
being previously unknown come with the novelty of
fiction. Sport, where it battles with the tigers of
India, the lions of Africa, or the buffalo in America—
with large game—is sure to be read with interest.
There does not appear to be much demand for history,
other than descriptions of great battles, not for history
in the modern sense. A good account of a battle, of
the actual fighting without the political movements
that led to it, is eagerly read. Almost perhaps more
than all these the wonders of science draw country
readers. If a little book containing an intelligible
and non-technical description of the electric railway
were offered in the villages, it would be certain to sell.
But it must not be educational in tone, because
they dislike to feel that they are being taught, and
they are repelled by books which profess to show
the reader how to do this or that. Technical books
are unsuitable; and as for the goody-goody, it is out
of the question. Most of the reading-rooms started in
villages by well-meaning persons have failed from the
introduction of goody-goody.

These are the principal subjects which the villager
would select or avoid had he the opportunity to make

a choice. As it is, he has to take what chance brings him, and often to be content with nothing, because he does not know what to ask for. If any one ever takes up the task of supplying the country with the sound and thoroughly first-class literature for which it is now ready, he will at least have the certain knowledge that he is engaged in a most worthy propaganda— with the likelihood of a large pecuniary reward. Such profits must of necessity be slow in the beginning, as they are in all new businesses, but they would also be slow in working off. It is a peculiarity of the country to be loyal. If country people believe in a bank, for instance—and they always believe in the first bank that comes among them—they continue to believe, and no effort whatever is necessary to keep the connection. It will be generations in dying out. So with a news-paper, so with an auctioneer—with everything. That which comes first is looked on with suspicion and dis-trust for a time, people are chary of having anything to do with it; but by-and-by they deal, and, having once dealt, always deal. They remain loyal; com-petition is of no use, the old name is the one believed in. Whoever acquires a name for the supply of the literature the country wants will retain that name for three-quarters of a century, and with a minimum of labour. At the same time the extent of country is so large that there is certainly room for several without clashing.

In working out a scheme for such a supply, it may be taken for granted that books intended for the villages must be cheap. When we consider the low prices at which reprinted books, the copyrights of which have expired, are now often met with, there really seems no difficulty in this. Sixpence, a shilling, eighteenpence; nothing must be more than two shillings, and a shilling should be the general maximum. For a shilling how many clever little books are on sale on London bookstalls! If so, why should not other books adapted to the villager's wishes be on sale at a similar price in the country? Something might, perhaps, be learned in this direction from the American practice. Books in America are often sold for a few cents; good-sized books too. Thousands of books are sold in France at a franc—twopence less than the maximum of a shilling. The paper is poor, the printing nothing to boast of, the binding merely paper, but the text is there. All the villager wants is the text. Binding, the face of the printing, the quality of the paper—to these outside accidents he is perfectly indifferent. If the text only is the object, a book can be produced cheaply. On first thoughts, it appeared that much might be effected in the way of reprinting extracts from the best authors, little handbooks which could be sold at a few pence. Something, indeed, might be done in this way. But upon the whole I think that as a general rule extracts are a mistake. There is nothing so unsatisfactory as an extract. You cannot supply the preceding part no the following with success. The extract itself loses its force and brilliance because the mind has not been prepared to perceive it by the gradual approach the author designed. It is like a face cut out of a large picture. The face may be pretty, but the meaning is lost. Such fragments of Shakspeare, for instance, as one sometimes still meets with reprinted in this way strike the mind like a fragment of rock hurled at one's head. They stun with rugged grandeur. As a rule, extracts, then, are a mistake—not as a rigid rule, but as a general principle. It would be better for the village reader to have a few books complete as to text, no matter how poorly printed, or how coarsely got up, than numerous partial reprints which lead the thoughts nowhere.

There must be no censorship, nothing kept back. The weakness and narrowness of mind which still exists—curious relic of the past—among some otherwise worthy classes who persist in thinking no one must read what they dislike, must not be permitted to domineer the village bookstall. There must be absolute freedom, or the villager will turn away. His mind, though open to receive, is robust like his body, and will not accept shackles. The propaganda should be of the best productions of the highest intellects, independent of creed and party. A practical difficulty arises from the copyrights; you cannot reprint a book of which the copyright still exists without injury to the original publisher and the author. But there are many hundred books of the very best order of which the copyright has expired, and which can be reprinted without injury to any one. Then there are the books which it may be presumed would be compiled on purpose for the object in view when once the scheme was in working order. Thirdly, it is probable that many living authors when about publishing a volume would not object to an arrangement for a production in cheap form after a reasonable time. So that there is no such difficulty here but that it might be overcome.

IV.—PLAN OF DISTRIBUTION.

When you have got your village library ready, how is it to be sold? How is it to be distributed an placed in the hands of the people? How are thes people to be got at? They are scattered far apart, and not within sound of trumpet. Travellers, indeed, could be sent round, but travellers cost money. There is the horse and the man to attend to it, turnpikes, repairs, hotels,—all the various expenses so well known in business. Each traveller could only call on a certain number of cottages and country houses per day, comparatively a small number, for they are often at long distances from each other; possibly he might find the garden gate locked and the people in the field. At the best after a long day's work he would only have sold a few dozen cheap books, and his inn bill would cover the profit upon them. Reduced thus to the rigid test of figures, the chance of success vanishes. But so, too, does the chance of success in any enterprise if looked at in this fashion. It must be borne in mind that the few copies of a cheap book sold in a day by a single traveller would not represent the ultimate possible return. The traveller prepares the ground which may yield a hundredfold afterwards. He awakens the demand and shows how it can be supplied. He teaches the villager what he wants, and how to get it. He lays the foundation of business in the future. The few pence he actually receives are the forerunners of pounds. Nothing can be accomplished without preliminary outlay. But conceding that the re ulation traveller is a costly instrument,

and putting that method upon one side for the present,
there are other means available. There is the post.
The post is a far more powerful disseminator in the
country than in town. A townsman picks up twenty
letters, snatches the envelopes open, and casts them
aside. The letters delivered in the country have
marvellously multiplied, but still country people do
not treat letters offhand. The arrival of a letter o
two is still an event; it is read twice or three times,
put in the pocket, and looked at again. Suburban residents receive circulars by every other post of every
kind and description, and cast them contemptuously
aside. In the country the delivery of a circular is not
so treated. It is certain to be read. Nothing may come
of it, but it is certain to be looked over, and more
than once. It will be left on the table, or be folded
up and put on the mantelpiece: it will not be destroyed.
Country people have not yet got into the habit which
may be called slur-reading. They really read. The
circulars at present delivered in the country are
counted by ones and twos where suburban residents get
scores and fifties. Almost the only firms who have
found out the value of circulars in the country are the
great drapery establishments, and their enterprise is
richly rewarded. The volume of business thus trans-
acted and brought to the London house by the circular
is enormous. There are very few farmhouses in the
country which do not contribute orders once or twice
a year. Very many families get all their materials
in this way, far cheaper, better, and more novel than
those on sale in the country towns. Here, then, is a
powerful lever ready to the hand of the publisher.

Every circular sent to a country house will be read
—not slurred—and will ultimately yield a return.
Cottagers never receive a circular at all. If a circular
came to a cottage by post it would be read and re-read,
folded up neatly, and preserved. After a time—for an
advertisement is exactly like seed sown in the ground
—something would be done. Some incident would
happen, and it would be remembered that there was
something about it in the circular—some book that
dealt with the subject. There is business directly.
The same post that brought the original circular, distributing knowledge of books, can bring the book
itself. Those who understand the importance attached
by country people, and especially by cottagers, to
anything that comes by post, will see the use of the
circular, which must be regarded as the most effective
means of reaching the rural population.

Next in value to the circular is the poster. The
extent to which posters are used in London, which
contains a highly educated population, is proof sufficient of its utility as a disseminator. But in the
country the poster has never yet been resorted to
as an aid to the bookseller. The auctioneers have
found out its importance, and their bills are freely
dispersed in every nook and corner. There are no
keener men, and they know from experience that it is
the cheapest way of advertising sales. Their posters
are everywhere—on walls, gate-posts, sign-posts, barns,
in the bars of wayside inns. The local drapers in the
market towns resort to the poster when they have a
sale at "vastly reduced" prices, sending round the
bill-sticker to remote hamlets and mere settlements of

two or three houses. They, too, know its value, an
that by it customers are attracted from the most out-
lying places. People in villages and hamlets pass the
greater part of their time out of doors and are in no
hurry, so that if in walking down the road to or from
their work they see a bill stuck upon a wall, they
invariably stop to read it. People on the London
railway platforms rather blink the posters displayed
around them : they would rather avoid them, though
they cannot altogether. It is just the reverse in the
hamlet, where the inhabitants lead such monotonous
lives, and have so little excitement that a fresh poster
is a good subject for conversation. No matter where
you put a poster, somebody will read it, and it is only
next in value to the circular, appealing to the public as
the circular appeals to the individual. Here are two
methods of reaching the country and of disseminating
a knowledge of books other than the employment of
expensive travellers. Even if travellers be called in,
circular and poster should precede their efforts.

There is then the advertisement column of the local
press. The local press has never been used for the
advertisement of such books as are suitable to country
readers, certainly not for the class hitherto chiefly
borne in view and for convenience designated villager.
The reason why such books have not been advertised
in the local press is probably because the authors and
publishers had no idea of the market that exists in the
country. For the most part readers in town and the
suburbs only glance at the exciting portions of papers,
and then cast them aside. Readers in the villages
read every line from the first column to the last, from

he title to the printer's address. The local papers are ploughed steadily through, just as the horses plough the fields, and every furrow conscientiously followed from end to end, advertisements and all. The brewer's, the grocer's, the draper's, the ironmonger's advertisements (market-town tradesmen), which have been there month after month, are all read, and the slightest change immediately noted. If there were any advertisement of books suitable to their taste it would be read in exactly the same manner. But in advertising for country people one fact must be steadily borne in mind—that they are slow to act; that is, the advertisement must be permanent. A few insertions are forgotten before those who have seen them have made up their minds to purchase. When an advertisement is always there, by-and-by the thought suggested acts on the will, and the stray coin is invested—it may be six months after the first inclination arose. The procrastination of country people is inexplicable to hurrying London men. But it is quite useless to advertise unless it is taken into account. If permanent, an advertisement in the local press will reach its mark. It is this permanency which gives another value to the circular and the poster; the circular is folded up and preserved to be looked at again like a book of reference; the poster remains on the dry wall of the barn, and the ink is legible months after it was first put up.

Having now informed the hamlets of the books which are in existence, if complete success is desired, the next step should be to put specimens of those books before the eyes of the residents. To read of

them, to know that they exist, and then to actually
see them—as Londoners see them in every street—
is a logical process leading to purchases. As already
pointed out, there are little shops in every village and
hamlet where the local paper can be obtained which
would gladly expose books for sale if the offer were
made to them. The same remark applies to the shops
in the market towns. These, too, require to be supplied; they require the thing explained to them, and
they would at once try it. Finally, let a traveller
once now and then come along, and call at these shops
to wake up and stir the business and change the face
of the counter. Let him while in the hamlet also call
at as many houses and cottages as he can manage in
a few hours, leaving circulars—always circulars—
behind him. There would then be a complete system
of supply.

SUNLIGHT IN A LONDON SQUARE.*

THERE are days now and again when the summer broods in Trafalgar Square; the flood of light from a cloudless sky gathers and grows, thickening the air; the houses enclose the beams as water is enclosed in a cup. Sideways from the white-painted walls light is reflected; upwards from the broad, heated pavement in the centre light and heat ascend; from the blue heaven it presses downwards. Not only from the sun —one point—but from the entire width of the visible blue the brilliant stream flows. Summer is enclosed between the banks of houses—all summer's glow and glory of exceeding brightness. The blue panel overhead has but a stray fleck of cloud, a Cupid drawn on the panel in pure white, but made indefinite by distance. The joyous swallows climb high into the illuminated air till the eye, daunted by the glow, can scarce detect their white breasts as they turn.

Slant shadows from the western side give but a margin of contrast; the rays are reflected through them, and they are only shadows of shadows. At the

* The sunlight and the winds enter London, and the life of the fields is there too, if you will but see it.

edges their faint sloping lines are seen in the air, where a million motes impart a fleeting solidity to the atmosphere. A pink-painted front, the golden eagle of the great West, golden lettering, every chance strip and speck of colour is washed in the dazzling light, made clear and evident. The hands and numerals of the clock yonder are distinct and legible, the white dial-plate polished; a window suddenly opened throws a flash across the square. Eastwards the air in front of the white walls quivers, heat and light reverberating visibly, and the dry flowers on the window sills burn red and yellow in the glare. Southwards green trees, far down the street, stand, as it seems, almost at the foot of the chiselled tower of Parliament—chiselled in straight lines and perpendicular grooves, each of which casts a shadow into itself. Again, the corners advanced before the main wall throw shadows on it, and the hollow casements draw shadows into their cavities. Thus, in the bright light against the blue sky the tower pencils itself with a dark crayon, and is built, not of stone, but of light and shadow. Flowing lines of water rise and fall from the fountains in the square, drooping like the boughs of a weeping ash, drifted a little to one side by an imperceptible air, and there sprinkling the warm pavement in a sparkling shower. The shower of finely divided spray now advances and now retreats, as the column of water bends to the current of air, or returns to its upright position.

By a pillared gateway there is a group in scarlet, and from time to time other groups in scarlet pass and repass within the barrack-court. A cream-tinted dress, a pink parasol—summer hues—go by in the stream of dark-clothed people; a flower fallen on the black water of a river. Either the light subdues the sound, or perhaps rather it renders the senses slumberous and less sensitive, but the great sunlit square is silent—silent, that is, for the largest city on earth. A slumberous silence of abundant light, of the full summer day, of the high flood of summer hours whose tide can rise no higher. A time to linger and dream under the beautiful breast of heaven, heaven brooding and descending in pure light upon man's handiwork. If the light shall thus come in, and of its mere loveliness overcome every aspect of dreariness, why shall not the light of thought, and hope—the light of the soul—overcome and sweep away the dust of our lives?

I stood under the portico of the National Gallery in the shade looking southwards, across the fountains and the lions, towards the green trees under the distant tower. Once a swallow sang in passing on the wing, garrulous still as in the time of old Rome and Augustan Virgil. From the high pediments dropped the occasional chatter of sparrows and the chirp of their young in the roofs. The second brood, they were late; they would not be in time for the harvest and the fields of stubble. A flight of blue pigeons rose from the central pavement to the level line of the parapet of the western houses. A starling shot across the square, swift, straight, resolute. I looked for the swifts, but they had gone, earliest of all to leave our sky for distant countries. Away in the harvest field the reaper, pausing in his work, had glanced up at the one stray

R

fleck of cloud in the sky, which to my fancy might be
a Cupid on a blue panel, and seeing it smiled in the
midst of the corn, wiping his blackened face, for he
knew it meant dry weather. Heat, and the dust of the
straw, the violent labour had darkened his face from
brown almost to blackness—a more than swarthiness,
a blackness. The stray cloud was spreading out in
filaments, each thread drawn to a fineness that ended
presently in disappearance. It was a sign to him of
continued sunshine and the prosperity of increased
wages. The sun from whose fiery brilliance I escaped
into the shadow was to him a welcome friend; his
neck was bare to the fierceness of the sun. His heart
was gladdened because the sky promised him permis-
sion to labour till the sinews of his fingers stiffened in
their crooked shape (as they held the reaping hook),
and he could hardly open them to grasp the loaf he
had gained.

So men laboured of old time, whether with plough
or sickle or pruning-hook, in the days when Augustan
Virgil heard the garrulous swallow, still garrulous.
An endless succession of labour, under the brightness
of summer, under the gloom of winter; to my thought
it is a sadness even in the colour and light and
glow of this hour of sun, this ceaseless labour, repeating
the furrow, reiterating the blow, the same furrow,
the same stroke—shall we never know how to
lighten it, how to live with the flowers, the swallows,
the sweet delicious shade, and the murmur of the
stream ? Not the blackened reaper only, but the
crowd whose low hum renders the fountain inaudible,
the nameless and unknown crowd of this immense city

wreathed round about the central square. I hope that
at some time, by dint of bolder thought and freer
action, the world shall see a race able to enjoy it
without stint, a race able to enjoy the flowers with
which the physical world is strewn, the colours of the
garden of life. To look backwards with the swallow
there is sadness, to-day with the fleck of cloud there
is unrest; but forward, with the broad sunlight, there
is hope.

Except you see these colours, and light, and tones,
except you see the blue heaven over the parapet,
you know not, you cannot feel, how great are the
possibilities of man. At my back, within the gallery,
there is many a canvas painted under Italian skies, in
glowing Spain, in bright Southern France. There are
scenes lit with the light that gleams on orange grove
and myrtle; there are faces tinted with the golden hue
that floats in southern air. But yet, if any one im-
partial will stand here outside, under the portico, and
forgetting that it is prosaic London, will look at the
summer enclosed within the square, and acknowledge
it for itself as it is, he must admit that the view—
light and colour, tone and shade—is equal to the
painted canvas, is full, as it were, to the brim of
interest, suggestion, and delight. Before the painted
canvas you stand with prepared mind; you have come
to see Italy, you are educated to find colour, and the
poetry of tone. Therefore you see it, if it is there.
Here in the portico you are unprepared, uneducated;
no one has ever given a thought of it. But now trace
out the colour and the brightness; gaze up into the
sky, watch the swallows, note the sparkle of the

fountain, observe the distant tower chiselled with the light and shade. Think, then, of the people, not as mere buyers and sellers, as mere counters, but as human beings—beings possessed of hearts and minds, full of the passions and the hopes and fears which made the ancient poets great merely to record. These are the same passions that were felt in antique Rome, whose very name is a section of human life. There is colour in these lives now as then.

VENICE IN THE EAST END.

THE great red bowsprit of an Australian clipper projects aslant the quay. Stem to the shore, the vessel thrusts an outstretched arm high over the land, as an oak in a glade pushes a bare branch athwart the opening. This beam is larger than an entire tree divested of its foliage, such trees, that is, as are seen in English woods. The great oaks might be bigger at the base where they swell and rest themselves on a secure pedestal. Five hundred years old an oak might measure more at six feet, at eight, or ten feet from the ground; after five hundred years, that is, of steady growth. But if even such a monarch were taken, and by some enormous mechanic power drawn out, and its substance elongated into a tapering spar, it would not be massive enough to form this single beam. Where it starts from the stem of the vessel it is already placed as high above the level of the quay as it is from the sward to the first branch of an oak. At its root it starts high overhead, high enough for a trapeze to be slung to it upon which grown persons could practise athletic exercises. From its roots, from the forward end of the deck, the red beam rises at a regular angle, diminishing in size with altitude till its end in comparison with the commencement may be called pointed, though in reality blunt. To the pointed end it would be a long climb; it would need a ladder. The dull red of the vast beam is obscured by the neutral tint of the ropes which are attached to it; colour generally gives a sense of lightness by defining shape, but this red is worn and weatherbeaten, rubbed and battered, so that its uncertain surface adds to the weight of the boom.

It hangs, an immense arm thrust across the sky; it is so high it is scarcely noticed in walking under it; it is so great and ponderous, and ultra in size, that the eye and mind alike fail to estimate it. For it is a common effect of great things to be overlooked. A moderately large rock, a moderately large house, is understood and mentally put down, as it were, at a certain figure, but the immense—which is beyond the human—cannot enter the organs of the senses. The portals of the senses are not wide enough to receive it; you must turn your back on it and reflect, and add a little piece of it to another little piece, and so build up your understanding. Human things are small; you live in a large house, but the space you actually occupy is very inconsiderable; the earth itself, great as it is, is overlooked, it is too large to be seen. The eye is accustomed to the little, and cannot in a moment receive the immense. Only by slow comparison with the bulk of oak trees, by the height of a trapeze, by the climbing of a ladder, can I convey to my mind a true estimate and idea of this gigantic bowsprit. It would be quite possible to walk by and never see it because of its size, as one walks by bridges or travels over a viaduct without a thought.

The vessel lies with her bowsprit projecting over the quay, moored as a boat run ashore on the quiet sandy beach of a lake, not as a ship is generally placed with her broadside to the quay wall or to the pier. Her stern is yonder—far out in the waters of the dock, too far to concern us much as we look from the verge of the wall. Access to the ship is obtained by a wooden staging running out at the side; instead of the ship lying beside the pier, a pier has been built out to fit to the ship. This plan, contrary to preconceived ideas, is evidently founded on good reason, for if such a vessel were moored broadside to the quay how much space would she take up ? There would be, first, the hull itself, say eighty yards, and then the immense bowsprit. Two or three such ships would, as it were, fill a whole field of water; they would fill a whole dock; it would not require many to cover a mile. By placing each stem to the quay they only occupy a space equal to their breadth instead of to their length. This arrangement, again, tends to deceive the eye; you might pass by, and, seeing only the bow, casually think there was nothing particular in it. Everything here is on so grand a scale that the largest component part is diminished; the quay, broad enough to build several streets abreast; the square, open stretches of gloomy water; and beyond these the wide river. The wind blows across these open spaces in a broad way—not as it comes in sudden gusts around a street corner, but in a broad open way,

each puff a quarter of a mile wide. The view of the
sky is open overhead, masts do not obstruct the
upward look; the sunshine illumines or the cloud-
shadows darken hundreds of acres at once. It is a
great plain; a plain of enclosed waters, built in and
restrained by the labour of man, and holding upon its
surface fleet upon fleet, argosy upon argosy. Masts
to the right, masts to the left, masts in front, masts
yonder above the warehouses; masts in among the
streets as steeples appear amid roofs; masts across the
river hung with drooping half-furled sails; masts afar
down thin and attenuated, mere dark straight lines
in the distance. They await in stillness the rising of
the tide.

It comes, and at the exact moment—foreknown to
a second—the gates are opened, and the world of ships
moves outwards to the stream. Downwards they
drift to the east, some slowly that have as yet but
barely felt the pull of the hawser, others swiftly, and
the swifter because their masts cross and pass the
masts of inward-bound ships ascending. Two lines of
masts, one raking one way, the other the other, cross
and puzzle the eye to separate their weaving motion
and to assign the rigging to the right vessel. White
funnels aslant, dark funnels, red funnels rush between
them; white steam curls upwards; there is a hum, a
haste, almost a whirl, for the commerce of the world
is crowded into the hour of the full tide. These great
hulls, these crossing masts a-rake, the intertangled
igging, the background of black barges drifting down-
ards, the lines and ripple of the water as the sun
comes out, if you look too steadily, daze the e es and

cause a sense of giddiness. It is so difficult to realize
so much mass—so much bulk—moving so swiftly, and
in so intertangled a manner; a mighty dance of
thousands of tons—gliding, slipping, drifting onwards,
yet without apparent effort. Thousands upon thousands of tons go by like shadows, silently, as if the
ponderous hulls had no stability or weight; like a
dream they float past, solid and yet without reality.
It is a giddiness to watch them.

This happens, not on one day only, not one tide, but
at every tide and every day the year through, year
after year. The bright summer sun glows upon it;
the red sun of the frosty hours of winter looks at it
from under the deepening canopy of vapour; the
blasts of the autumnal equinox howl over the vast
city and whistle shrilly in the rigging; still at every
tide the world of ships moves out into the river. Why
does not a painter come here and place the real
romance of these things upon canvas, as Venice has
been placed? Never twice alike, the changing
atmosphere is reflected in the hue of the varnished
masts, now gleaming, now dull, now dark. Till it has
been painted, and sung by poet, and described by
writers, nothing is human. Venice has been made
human by poet, painter, and dramatist, yet what was
Venice to this—this the Fact of our own day? Two
of the caravels of the Doge's fleet, two of Othello's
strongest war-ships, could scarcely carry the mast of
my Australian clipper. At a guess it is four feet
through; it is of iron, tubular; there is room for a
winding spiral staircase within it; as for its height, I
will not risk a guess at it. Could Othello's war-ships

carry it they would consider it a feat, as the bringing
of the Egyptian obelisk to London was thought a feat.
The petty ripples of the Adriatic, what were they?
This red bowsprit at its roots is high enough to
suspend a trapeze; at its head a ladder would be
required to mount it from the quay; yet by-and-by,
when the tide at last comes, and its time arrives to
move outwards in the dance of a million tons, this
mighty bowsprit, meeting the Atlantic rollers in the
Bay of Biscay, will dip and bury itself in foam under
the stress of the vast sails aloft. The forty-feet
billows of the Pacific will swing these three or four
thousand or more tons, this giant hull which must be
moored even stem to shore, up and down and side to
side as a handful in the grasp of the sea. Now, each
night as the clouds part, the north star looks down
upon the deck; then, the Southern Cross will be
visible in the sky, words quickly written, but half a
globe apart. What was there in Venice to arouse
thoughts such as spring from the sight of this red
bowsprit? In two voyages my Australian clipper
shall carry as much merchandise as shall equal the
entire commerce of Venice for a year.

Yet it is not the volume, not the bulk only;
cannot you see the white sails swelling, and the
proud vessel rising to the Pacific billows, the north
star sinking, and the advent of the Southern Cross;
the thousand miles of ocean without land around, the
voyage through space made visible as sea, the far, far
south, the transit around a world? If Italian painters
had had such things as these to paint, if poets of old
time had had such things as these to sing, do you

imagine they would have been contented with crank caravels and tales thrice told already? They had eyes to see that which was around them. Open your eyes and see those things which are around us at this hour.

THE PIGEONS AT THE BRITISH MUSEUM.

THE front of the British Museum stands in the sunlight clearly marked against the firm blue of the northern sky. The blue appears firm as if solid above the angle of the stonework, for while looking towards it—towards the north—the rays do not come through the azure, which is therefore colour without life. It seems nearer than the southern sky, it descends and forms close background to the building; as you approach you seem to come nearer to the blue surface rising at its rear. The dark edges of sloping stone are distinct and separate, but not sharp; the hue of the stone is toned by time and weather, and is so indefinite as to have lost its hardness. Those small rounded bodies upon the cornice are pigeons resting in the sun, so motionless and neutral-tinted that they might be mistaken for some portion of the carving. A double gilt ring, a circle in a circle, at the feet of an allegorical figure gleams brightly against the dark surface. The sky already seems farther away seen between th boles of stone, perpetual shade dwells in their depth, but two or three of the pigeons fluttering down are searchin for food on the sunlit gravel at the bottom of the steps. To them the building is merely a rock, pierced with convenient caverns; they use its exterior for their purpose, but penetrate no farther. With air and light, the sunlit gravel, the green lawn between it and the outer railings—with these they are concerned, and with these only. The heavy roll of the traffic in Oxford Street, audible here, is nothing to them; the struggle for money does not touch them, they let it go by. Nor the many minds searching and re-searching in the great Library, this mental toil is no more to them than the lading of the waggons in the street. Neither the tangible product nor the intellectual attainment is of any value—only the air and light. There are idols in the galleries within upon whose sculptured features the hot Eastern sun shone thousands of years since. They were made by human effort, however mistaken, and they were the outcome of human thought and handiwork. The doves fluttered about the temples in those days, full only of the air and light. They fluttered about the better temples of Greece and round the porticos where philosophy was born. Still only the light, the sunlight, the air of heaven. We labour on and think, and carve our idols and the pen never ceases from its labour; but the lapse of the centuries has left us in the same place. The doves who have not laboured nor travailed in thought possess the sunlight. Is not theirs the preferable portion?

The shade deepens as I turn from the portico to the hall and vast domed house of books. The half-hearted light under the dome is stagnant and dead. For it is the nature of light to beat and throb; it has a

pulse and undulation like the swing of the sea. Under
the trees in the woodlands it vibrates and lives; on
the hills there is a resonance of light. It beats against
every leaf, and, thrown back, beats again; it is agitated
with the motion of the grass blades; you can feel it
ceaselessly streaming on your face. It is renewed and
fresh every moment, and never twice do you see the
same ray. Stayed and checked by the dome and
book-built walls, the beams lose their elasticity, and
the ripple ceases in the motionless pool. The eyes,
responding, forget to turn quickly, and only partially
see. Deeper thought and inspiration quit the heart,
for they can only exist where the light vibrates and
communicates its tone to the soul. If any imagine
they shall find thought in many books, certainly they
will be disappointed. Thought dwells by the stream
and sea, by the hill and in the woodland, in the sunlight and free wind, where the wild dove haunts.
Walls and roof shut it off as they shut off the undulation of light. The very lightning cannot penetrate
here. A murkiness marks the coming of the cloud,
and the dome becomes vague, but the fierce flash is
shorn to a pale reflection, and the thunder is no more
than the rolling of a heavier truck loaded with tomes.
But in closing out the sky, with it is cut off all that
the sky can tell you with its light, or in its passion of
storm.

Sitting at these long desks and trying to read, I soon
find that I have made a mistake; it is not here I shall
find that which I seek. Yet the magic of books draws
me here time after time, to be as often disappointed.
Something in a book tempts the mind as pictures

tempt the eye; the eye grows weary of pictures, but looks again. The mind wearies of books, yet cannot forget that once when they were first opened in youth they gave it hope of knowledge. Those first books exhausted, there is nothing left but words and covers. It seems as if all the books in the world—really books —can be bought for £10. Man's whole thought is purchaseable at that small price, for the value of a watch, of a good dog. For the rest it is repetition and paraphrase. The grains of wheat were threshed out and garnered two thousand years since. Except the receipts of chemists, except specifications for the steam-engine, or the electric motor, there is nothing in these millions of books that was not known at the commencement of our era. Not a thought has been added. Continual threshing has widened out the heap of straw and spread it abroad, but it is empty. Nothing will ever be found in it. Those original grains of true thought were found beside the stream, the sea, in the sunlight, at the shady verge of woods. Let us leave this beating and turning-over of empty straw; let us return to the stream and the hills; let us ponder by night in view of the stars.

It is pleasant to go out again into the portico under the great columns. On the threshold I feel nearer knowledge than when within. The sun shines, and southwards above the houses there is a statue crowning the summit of some building. The figure is in the midst of the light; it stands out clear and white as if in Italy. The southern blue is luminous—the beams of light flow through it—the air is full of the undulation and life of light. There is rest in gazing at the sky: a sense that wisdom does exist and may be found, a hope returns that was taken away among the books. The green lawn is pleasant to look at, though it is mown so ruthlessly. If they would only let the grass spring up, there would be a thought somewhere entangled in the long blades as a dewdrop sparkles in their depths. Seats should be placed here, under the great columns or by the grass, so that one might enjoy the sunshine after books and watch the pigeons. They have no fear of the people, they come to my feet, but the noise of a door heavily swinging-to in the great building alarms them; they rise and float round, and return again. The sunlight casts a shadow of the pigeon's head and neck upon his shoulder; he turns his head, and the shadow of his beak falls on his breast. Iridescent gleams of bronze and green and blue play about his neck; blue predominates. His pink feet step so near, the red round his eye is visible. As he rises vertically, forcing his way in a straight line upwards, his wings almost meet above his back and again beneath the body; they are put forth to his full stroke. When his flight inclines and becomes gradually horizontal, the effort is less and the wing tips do not approach so closely.

They have not laboured in mental searching as we have; they have not wasted their time looking among empty straw for the grain that is not there. They have been in the sunlight. Since the days of ancient Greece the doves have remained in the sunshine; we who have laboured have found nothing. In the sunshine, by the shady verge of woods, by the sweet waters where the wild dove sips, there alone will thought be found.

THE PLAINEST CITY IN EUROPE.

THE fixed perspective of Paris neither elongates nor contracts with any change of atmosphere, so that the apparent distance from one point to another remains always the same. Reduced to the simplest elements the street architecture of Paris consists of two parallel lines, which to the eye appear to gradually converge. In sunshine and shade the sides of the street approach in an unvarying ratio; a cloud goes over, and the lines do not soften; brilliant light succeeds, and is merely light — no effect accompanies it. The architecture conquers, and is always architecture; it resists the sun, the air, the rain, being without expression. The geometry of the street can never be forgotten. Moving along it you have merely advanced so far along a perspective, between the two lines which tutors rule to teach drawing. By-and-by, when you reach the other end and look back, the perspective is accurately reversed. This is now the large end of the street, and that which has been left the small. The houses seen from this end present precisely the same façade as they did at starting, so that were it not for the sense of weariness from walking it would be easy to imagine that no movement had taken place. Each

s

house is exactly the same height as the next, the windows are of the same pattern, the wooden outer blinds the same shape; the line of the level roof runs along straight and unbroken, the chimneys are either invisible or insignificant. Nothing projects, no bow window, balcony, or gable; the surface is as flat as well can be. From parapet to pavement the wall descends plumb, and the glance slips along it unchecked. Each house is exactly the same colour as the next, white; the wooden outer blinds are all the same colour, a dull grey; in the windows there are no visible red, or green, or tapestry curtains, mere sashes. There are no flowers in the windows to catch the sunlight. The upper stories have the air of being uninhabited, as the windows have no curtains whatever, and the wooden blinds are frequently closed. Two flat vertical surfaces, one on each side of the street, each white and grey, extend onwards and approach in mathematical ratio. That is a Parisian street.

Go on now to the next street, and you find precisely the same conditions repeated—the streets that cross are similar, those that radiate the same. Some are short, others long, some wide, some narrow; they are all geometry and white paint. The vast avenues, a rifle-shot across, such as the Avenue de l'Opéra, differ only in width and in the height of the houses. The monotony of these gigantic houses is too great to be expressed. Then across the end of the avenue they throw some immense facade—some public building, an opera-house, a palace, a ministry, anything will do—in order that you shall see nothing but Paris.

Weary of the gigantic monotony of the gigantic houses,
exactly alike, your eye shall not catch a glimpse of
some distant cloud rising like a snowy mountain (as
Japanese artists show the top of Fusiyama); you shall
not see the breadth of the sky, nor even any steeple,
tower, dome, or gable; you shall see nothing but Paris;
the avenue is wide enough for the Grand Army to
march down, but the exit to the eye is blocked by
this immense meaningless facade drawn across it. No
doubt it is executed in the "highest style;" in effect
it appears a repetition of windows, columns, and door-
ways exactly alike, all quite meaningless, for the
columns support nothing, like the fronts sold in boxes
of children's toy bricks. Perhaps on the roof there is
some gilding, and you ask yourself the question why
it is there. These façades, of which there are so many,
vary in detail; in effect they are all the same, an utter
weariness to the eye. Every fresh day's research into
the city brings increasing disappointment, a sense of
the childish, of feebleness, and weakness exhibited in
public, as if they had built in sugar for the top of a
cake. The level ground will not permit of any advantage of view; there are none of those sudden views so
common and so striking in English towns. Everything is planed, smoothed, and set to an oppressive
regularity.

Turning round a corner one comes suddenly on a
pillar of a dingy, dull hue, whose outline bulges
unpleasantly. In London you would shrug your
shoulders, mutter "hideous!" and pass on. This is the
famous Vendôme Column. As for the Column of July,
it is so insignificant, so silly (no other word expresses

it so well), that a second glance is carefully avoided. The Hôtel de Ville, a vast white building, is past description, it is so plain and so repellent in its naked glaring assertion. From about old Notre Dame they have removed every mediæval outwork which had grown up around and rendered it lifelike; it now rises perpendicular and abrupt from the white surface of the square. Unless you had been told that it was the Notre Dame of Victor Hugo you would not look at its exterior twice. The interior is another matter. In external form Notre Dame cannot enter into competition with Canterbury. The barrack-like Hôtel des Invalides, the tomb of Napoleon—was ever a tomb so miserably lacking in all that should inspire a reverential feeling ?

The marble tub in which the urn is sunk, the gilded chapel, and the yellow windows—could anything be more artificial and less appropriate ? They jar on the senses, they insult the torn flags which were carried by the veterans at Austerlitz, and which now droop, never again to be unfurled to the wind of battle. The tiny Seine might as well flow in a tunnel, being bridged so much. There remains but the Arc de Triomphe, the only piece of architecture in all modern Paris worth a second look. Even this is spoiled by the same intolerable artificiality. The ridiculous sculpture on the face, the figures blowing trumpets, and, above all, the group on the summit, which the tongue of man cannot describe, so utterly hideous is it, destroy the noble lines of the arch, if any one is so imprudent as to approach near it. Receding down the Avenue Friedland—somewhat aslant—the chestnut trees presently conceal the side sculpture ; and then by tilting one's hat so that the brim shall hide the group on the summit, it is possible to admire the proportions of the Arc. In the Tuileries gardens there is a spot where distance obliterates the sculpture, and the projecting bough of an elm conceals the group on the top. Here the arch appears noble ; but it is no longer French ; it is now merely a copy of a Roman original, which any of our own architects could erect for us in Hyde Park. For the most part the vaunted Boulevards are but planted with planes, the least pleasing of trees, whose leaves present an unvarying green, till they drop a dead brown ; and the horse-chestnuts in the Champs Elysées are set in straight lines to repeat the geometry of the streets.

Thus central Paris has no character. It is without individuality and expressionless. Suppose you said, "The human face is really very irregular ; it requires shaping. This nose projects ; here, let us flatten it to the level of the cheek. This mouth curves at the corners ; let us cut it straight. These eyebrows arch ; make them straight. This colour is too flesh-like ; bring white paint. Besides, the features move, they laugh, they assume sadness ; this is wrong. Here, divide the muscles, that they may henceforth remain in unvarying rigidity." That is what has been done to Paris. It is made straight ; it is idealized after Euclid ; it is stiff, wearisome, and feeble. Lastly, it has no expression. The distances as observed at the commencement remain always the same, partly because of the obtrusive eometry and the monotony, partly because of the whiteness, and partly because of the peculiarity of the atmosphere, for which of course the Parisian is not responsible, but should have remembered in building. Advantage might surely have been taken of so clear an air in some manner. The colour and tone, the light and shade, the change and variety of London are entirely wanting; in short, Paris is the plainest city in Europe.

LaVergne, TN USA
24 November 2010
206118LV00002B/24/P